SCOTTISH TRADITIONS

AND

FESTIVALS

Raymond Lamont-Brown

Chambers

Published 1991 by W&R Chambers Ltd,
43–45 Annandale Street, Edinburgh EH7 4AZ

British Library Cataloguing in Publication Data
Lamont-Brown, Raymond
   Traditions and festivals of Scotland. – (Chambers mini
   guides).
   1. Scottish calendar customs
   I. Title
   394.269411

ISBN 0-550-20062-2

Illustrations by John Haxby and Janet MacKay
Cover design by John Marshall

Typeset by Bookworm Typesetting Ltd, Edinburgh
Printed in Singapore by
Singapore National Printers Ltd

Contents

Preface

Scotland has a wealth of traditions, festivals and customs that add colour and interest to the life of the nation. Many have their roots in ancient Pictish rituals and Scandinavian myth. Others are more modern and associated with particular people or events, some are almost forgotten. All are fascinating.

Surprisingly very little has been written about such Scottish events and practices outside academic studies. To the folklorists, collectors and authors of these volumes, the present writer gives grateful thanks. The purpose of this book, however, is to provide a popular introduction to the festive Scottish year.

Stringent efforts have been made to ensure that the information in this book is correct at time of going to press. However, as many events are organized by voluntary clubs, associations and committees, their listing is no guarantee that such events will take place; further, time, place, date and format of events may change annually at the direction of the organizers. To avoid disappointment, readers are urged to enquire of local organizations on the likelihood of events taking place before specifically setting out to attend such functions. Neither the publishers, nor the author can be held responsible for the change of location of events, or their cancellation.

Introduction

The lifestyle of Scots was once closely bounded by the hedges of the village fields, the drovers' tracks over the moors, and the vast expanses of forest. In the fields they cleared stones, ploughed, harrowed, singled and harvested. Down the tracks they drove their sheep and cows, and in the forests they gathered firewood, herbs and acorns. And all these activities were governed by the rhythm of the seasons.

As candles and paraffin lamps were the only source of artificial light, Scots tended to bed early and rise betimes. Except for Sunday, a universal holiday, working hours were from sunrise to sunset. Through all this was clearly seen the governing hand of nature, for even a visit to a nearby town generally coincided with a market or fair. Pleasure, too, was usually found in the context of the seasonal work programme. For many centuries an agrarian country, the Scottish farming cycle evolved its own customs, traditions and festivals. Life fell naturally into a calendar extant since Celtic times (and only later Christianized).

Scottish custom was founded on the old Celtic quarter-days of Imbolc (1 February), Beltane (1 May), Lugnasad (1 August), and Samhuinn (1 November). On to Imbolc, the Celtic lambing festival, was grafted Candlemas; Beltane, the fire festival of the spring equinox, became May Day; Lugnasad, the festival of 1 August named in favour of the Celtic hero Lugh Lamh Fadn, became the feast of the first fruits; while Samhuinn developed as Hallowe'en (Martinmas). And this book tells of the extant festivals of these seasons.

Once every Scottish custom, tradition and festival had its complicated ritual. The whole realm of superstition was brought alive during the round of Scottish traditional customs. At Hallowe'en, for instance, the devil and his minions stalked the unwary; at Hogmanay the beasts of the field were deemed to have the power of speech for as long as it took the church bells to strike twelve – and could be petitioned for advice; and at any of the season's festivals all had to be careful not to upset the spirits of Scottish Elfame. Rowan twigs were braided into the tails and manes of animals to keep demons away; parsley was planted and horse-shoes nailed above doors to thwart witches; and no woman dare whistle lest she raise a storm to interfere with the smooth running of the seasons' rituals. For as the seasons met and merged, mankind was at his most vulnerable.

As in all things the Scots have had their own way of celebrating acts and events, from bank holidays to leap years:

BANK HOLIDAYS

The Bank Holiday Act was passed in 1871, and established such holidays as Easter Monday and Box-ing Day. They were introduced to relieve the toil of the Victorian masses. It took about a year for Scots folk to take them seriously. The inventor is said to have been Sir John Lubbock, MP for Maidstone. Although Lubbock was an Englishman he had a great interest in Scotland and was Rector of St Andrews University in 1907. It was Lubbock who established the modern aspects of the Bank Holiday in Scotland.

Although called 'Bank' holiday, the shrewd sponsor intended the Bill to cover all places of work – to have proposed a 'Public Holidays Bill' would have invited opposition from mill-owners and other major indus-trial employers. Indeed, there was opposition to such holidays in Scotland, particularly from the temperance societies who said they would encourage increased drunkenness, especially at railway terminals. And the strong Presbyterians thought that such holidays would lead to vandalism and promiscuity. Up to the 1871 Act there were very few holidays in Scotland compared to today. The 1833 Factory Act laid down that workers over the age of eighteen should have eight annual half-holidays. By 1850 the Saturday half-holiday had been instituted, but it was not until the turn of the century that it became the norm. The 'monthly holiday' was a very popular event in Scottish villages with buses 'got up' to visit the big cities.

The basic Scots holiday originated in medieval times and they were started by the religious (holiday = holy day). Because of their religious origins many fairs and markets were held on saints' days, from St Matthew's Fair, Cumnock (21 September) to the eight-day All Hallows Fair at Edinburgh (31 October). Some of the fairs come down to us with strange names like the March Seed Thursday at Biggar and the June Scythe Fair at Old Cumnock. The atmosphere of the fairs was made up of noise, bustle, confusion and colour to stimulate the senses. One of the best ways to get the flavour of the old-time market is to look at Sir David Wilkie's picture *Pitlessie Fair* of 1804, wherein he painted 104 faces of the folk who attended this Fife fair of May and October. Such events were a great opportunity to gossip and were attended by cattle-dealers, horse-coupers, hawkers, pedlars, pickpockets, whores, travelling merchants, and drovers and their dogs.

THE OLD SCOTS LEAP YEAR

The word 'leap' comes from the Old Norse *hlauper* indicating a jump forward, and the term originates from the fact that in a leap year a fixed festival falls on the next weekday but one to that of a normal year (that is it 'leaps' over a day). It is needed to compensate for the discrepancy between the calendar year of 365 days and the astronomical year of 365.242 days and is applied whenever the year is divisible by four as in 1992, 1996 and 2000. In 45 BC the calendar was reformed by Julius Caesar on the advice of the Egyptian astronomer Sosigenes. This was used throughout Europe until 1582 when Pope Gregory XIII was told by astronomers that the calendar was getting ahead of itself. So to cut a long story short, an extra day was added and Scotland changed to the new reckoning in 1600 (except St Kilda), but the changes were only made in England in 1752.

The custom that women should be able to propose to men only in a leap year comes from a most unlikely legend. It is said that St Patrick invented it following a riot in St Bridget's nunnery, where the women demanded the right to propose marriage. Why nuns should want to do this is vague, but they might have had the whole of womankind in mind. So, St Patrick agreed that there should be a leap year, and thus the idea was established. Victorian chronicles gave credence to a so-called law passed by the Scottish parliament in 1228, stating that if a man refused to marry the woman he had proposed to he could be fined £100; if he did refuse, he had to pay his fine and present the woman with a silk gown.

At one time Leap Year was an official festival in Scotland and it fell on the octave of the Feast of St Oswald, Archbishop of York, who died in 992; he was the most unfortunate of the saints as he only received a feast in Scotland every four years. In Scotland on 29 February several of the old grammar schools gave their pupils one hour (between three and four in the afternoon) to drink beer and wine. There was much superstition attached to the Scottish Leap Year: from Peeblesshire there was the old saying, 'A leap year is never good for sheep', and in neighbouring Selkirkshire they said that broad beans would grow the wrong way. People's characters would change at this time too, they said in the west of Scotland, and it was universally deemed an unlucky day because the old folk said the number 29 denoted treachery and uncertainty. Dr David Rorie noted in Victorian Auchterderran, Fife, that Leap Year was considered 'unlucky for beasts and bodies', and, 'there's a heap o' witchcraft gaun aboot at Leap Year.'

PROFESSIONAL CUSTOMS

No doubt taking their lead from the customs and festivals associated with the old trade guilds of Scotland, the professions also had their customs, particularly the legal profession. One example is to be seen in the writings of John Lamont of Newton who, writing in his diary of 1649–71, tells of the custom of 'wife's interest'. It seems that it was a custom for a buyer of land to present the seller's lady with a ring, or some small token or a money gift. Undoubtedly this stems from the old pagan rites of placating the gods with votive offerings, or giving a bounty to a shaman.

WILL SCOTLAND'S TRADITIONS, CUSTOMS AND FESTIVALS SURVIVE?

Alas, more than two-thirds of Scotland's old customs, from St Serf's Festival at Culross, Fife, to Dingwall's Burning of the Crate, have died out. Others remain only in relic, and today, with the five-day working week and month or so of statutory holidays, the need for breaks from work disguised as vibrant, colourful saints' days has passed. Modern man and woman have expunged the calendar of many festive days. Whitsun is now eclipsed by the Spring Bank Holiday and May Day is an excuse for political mummery. The bonfires of Samhuinn, later associated with St Martin, have now come to celebrate the attempted regicide of Guido Fawkes. Even so, the ubiquitous Guy seems to be having a steady decline of his own.

Still there are some community-minded folk who are trying to revive the old customs, like the rehabilitation of the Anstruther Fishermen's Queen, and to keep alive those customs which survived to the twentieth century. Modern materialistic and all-knowing society has suffocated that sure instinct which our ancestors had for holding on to anything that served an occult practical purpose. In letting that happen we have lost much community fun and have denied succeeding generations their true links with the pulsating heritage of Scottish custom, tradition and festival. Yet, is there light at the end of the tunnel? Arts societies and local tourist authorities are seeing the potential of festivals and traditions, and from Pittenweem to Portsoy more time is being given over to festival weeks and gala days. This is a good trend, but there is a long way to go until Scotland is rich in the seasonal festivities which once echoed through the streets.

Since its inception in 1947 the Edinburgh International Festival of Music and Drama (held for three weeks at the end of August) has dominated Scotland's cultural life. Following 1990, however, and in particular the elevation of Glasgow into 'The Cultural Capital of

Europe' and a year of festivities in Scotland's second city, there might be a new renaissance of the nation's traditions, festivals and customs.

WHERE TO OBTAIN BASIC INFORMATION

This book is a distillation of the customs and festivals of the past, with an interlarding of the new. Today in June alone there are over 125 official festivals in Scotland, with as many local events which receive little national coverage; consequently much pruning has been needed for this volume to offer a representative selection. New tourist information centres are opening all the time, but as a starting point these regional tourist authorities may be contacted for festival programmes and approached for addresses of more local information offices:

Borders: Scottish Borders Tourist Board, Murray's Green, Jedburgh, TD8 6BE tel: 0835 63435

Dumfries and Galloway: Dumfries and Galloway Tourist Board, Campbell House, Bankend Road, Dumfries DG1 4TH tel: 0387 50434

Midlothian: Chief Librarian, Midlothian District Council, 7 Station Road, Roslin, Midlothian EH25 9PF tel: 031-440 2210

Edinburgh: Tourist Information Centre, Waverley Market, 3 Princes Street, Edinburgh EH2 2QP tel: 031-557 1700

West Lothian, Falkirk and Dunfermline: Forth Valley Tourist Board, Burgh Halls, The Cross, Linlithgow, West Lothian EH49 7AH tel: 0506 844600

East Lothian: East Lothian Tourist Board, Brunton Hall, Musselburgh, East Lothian EH21 6AE tel: 0368 63353

Strathclyde: Greater Glasgow Tourist Board, 35–39 St Vincent Place, Glasgow G1 2ER tel: 041-204 4400

Fife: St Andrews and North East Fife Tourist Board, 2 Queens Gardens, St Andrews, Fife KY16 9TE tel: 0334 72021

Central: Loch Lomond, Stirling and Trossachs Tourist Board, 41 Dumbarton Road, Stirling FK8 2QQ tel: 0786 75019

Tayside: City of Dundee Tourist Board, 4 City Square, Dundee DD1 3BA   tel: 0382 23141

Grampian: Aberdeen Tourist Information Centre, St Nicholas House, Broad Street, Aberdeen AB9 1DE tel: 0224 642121

Highlands and Islands: High-line, Station Road, Dingwall, Ross-shire IV15 9JE   tel: 0349 63434

Scottish Tourist Board: 23 Ravelston Terrace, Edinburgh EH4 3EU   tel: 031-332 2433

1

New Year and the Feasts of the Virgin Year

1 JANUARY

New Year's Day/Ne'erday

As the last bell tolls in kirk and tollbooth to welcome the infant year, Scotland settles down to a round of celebrations that are centuries old. It was James VI and I's decree in Privy Council at Holyrood Palace in December 1599 that made 1 January the beginning of the legal year in Scotland. This changed it from 25 March and fixed it around the merrymaking every Scot remembers more than Christmas. Indeed, up to modern times Christmas Day was a working day in Scotland. As a preamble to New Year's Day, though, there was a great 'redding-up' when the house was given a good cleaning and all the domestic jobs from winding clocks to darning socks were carried out, to go into the New Year with no chores undone – or at least that was the theory.

In medieval Scotland, before the Reformation, devotions were centred on the *Circumcisio Domini* (the Feast of the Circumcision of Our Lord). And, be it 25 March or 1 January, it was long the custom to gather at a nearby prehistoric site (a stone circle maybe) or at the mercat cross, to welcome publicly the New Year. The most tenacious of Scotland's old New Year's Day ceremonies, of course, is first-footing.

First-Footing

The ritual round of visiting friends and neighbours to give them shortbread and their 'New Year' from the family 'bottle', dates back to the days when the medieval clergy took bread, cheese and wine to the poor, itself a relic of pagan food offerings instead of a human sacrifice to the gods of the seasons.

The first visitor to a house on New Year's Day was

the first-foot, who brought the quality of good luck to the house and family for the ensuing year. To assure that the host family would not go hungry, a small gift of cake (handsel) or bread was brought. Among the gifts might also be a piece of coal to symbolize a year's warmth, and salt to represent wealth. In many places in Scotland the first-foot carried an evergreen twig to represent the continuance of life. Various parts of the country had gifts to suit the locality – red herrings in Dundee to symbolize a good sea harvest, or a wheat sheaf in Galloway to attract good crops.

Because he was a bringer of luck, the choice of the first-foot was important. It was always the role of a man, for, as with her presence on a fishing boat, a woman was deemed exceedingly unlucky. The first-foot must never be flat-footed or cross-eyed, or have eyebrows that met across the nose: these were symbols of the evil eye and indeed all with congenital disability were feared as first-foots. Usually the first-foot was dark and never fair, or, worst of all, red-haired: this was a superstitious relic of the days when Scotland's coasts were raided by the red-haired Norsemen. Those who had no first-foot might share one with the street or parish, or at the stroke of twelve just open the front door and bid welcome entry to the New Year. Should the worst happen – a call by a first-foot who had any of the bad luck omens – the evil fortune could be averted by casting a pinch of salt into the fire or placing a rowan-twig cross tied with red thread above the door to neutralize the evil. For everyone knew the old saw: 'Rowan twig and red thread gar the witches tine their speed.'

In country districts animals were not left out of the New Year visits. On New Year's morning a farmer gave his animals an extra sheaf of corn as Robert Burns reminds us in his poem, 'The Auld Farmer's New-Year Morning Salutation to his Auld Mare, Maggie' (1785–6):

> A Guid New-Year I wish thee, Maggie!
> Hae, there's a ripp to thy auld baggie:
> > *handful from sheaf/belly*

Often the farmer's wife would take sheaves of corn to each of the cottages of the farmer's workers for their own beasts, with a gift or two for each family. Many farmers held open-house on New Year's morning, giving breakfast to friends and workers.

Kissing

As the day of goodwill it has long been a custom to kiss the opposite sex for 'good luck' on New Year's Day. Modern fashions of hygiene and fear of public abuse of women has led to the dying out of indiscriminate public kissing at New Year, but one observer of 1857 wrote:

> The young women walk about the streets [of Edinburgh] without fear as nobody thinks of interfering with them in the way of salutation till the town clock warns of the approach of twelve. Within a few minutes of that hour, young women of all ranks may be seen creeping along close to the wall, thinking to gain their houses without being discovered; young men may also be seen moving after them, only waiting for the warning clock in order to make the salute which cannot be rejected . . . even a lady who passes in a sedan chair or a carriage submits with the best grace she can, to pay a forfeit she has incurred. With the kiss and the handshake comes 'A gude New Year tae ye', or *Slàinte mhòr* (Good

health), or *Bliadhna sona* (A happy New Year) in Gaelic.

The Het Pint

In medieval times at the abbeys and priories up and down the length of Scotland, on New Year's Day a huge bowl (the *poculum caritatis*) was set before the abbot. After he had drunk from it, all sipped a celebration to the New Year and to each other in order of succession in the abbey. From this custom comes the Scottish Het Pint.

At every ingle-neuk in Scotland, at the approach of twelve o'clock, the Het Pint was prepared. A kettle of warm, sweetened and spiced ale, with an infusion of spirits, was made ready and when the 'toon clock' had pealed the knell of the dead year, each member of the family drank from the steamy brew. And then off they would go to visit relations with the rest of the Het Pint. An alternative in the north of Scotland to the spice and whisky Het Pint was the imbibing of *swata*, a beverage made from the soaked husks of oats with honey and whisky. In the Highlands they had their Athole Brose (whisky, honey, oatmeal and cream).

The traditional food to go with the Het Pint was the oat bannock; shortbread (relic of the ancient Yule cake) which varied in its local recipe; and black bun, Scotland's traditional Twelfth Night cake of dried fruit, nuts and spices in a pastry case. In Scotland up to modern times, New Year's Day was the day for the family feast of goose, or steak pie and plum pudding or clootie-dumpling.

Auld Lang Syne

This is the traditional New Year song, sung as the company are ranged in a circle holding hands. The original author of the song is unknown and its wording has been reworked by various writers like Sir Robert Ayton and Allan Ramsay, but the version sung today (although mangled by modern slips of memory) was that reworked by Robert Burns for James Johnson's *Scots Musical Museum* (completed 1803). Here is Burns's version of the first verse and chorus to the tune known since 1700:

Should auld acquaintance be forgot,
And never brought to mind?
Should auld acquaintance be forgot,
And auld lang syne.

Chorus: For auld lang syne, my dear,
For auld lang syne,
We'll tak' a cup o' kindness yet,
For auld lang syne.

Football, curling and rugby matches take place on New Year's Day in Scotland and the various fixtures are advertised in the local press. And there's *camanachd* (shinty) in the Highlands.

Boys' and Men's Ba' Games, Kirkwall, Orkney

Two ball games are played in the Norse-founded town of Kirkwall, Orkney, on New Year's Day (and Christmas Day): the Boys' Ba' game during the morning and the Men's Ba' game during the afternoon. The players are divided into two opposing teams, the Up-the-Gates (Uppies) and the Doon-the-Gates (Doonies), and qualification to play was once regulated by place of birth in the town; 'gates' taking its origins from the old Scots *gait*, a street. The dividing line for the game's location is the lane opposite the Cathedral of St Magnus which separates the Old Burgh from Laverock (Upper Town). By necessity the town's shops are barricaded throughout the festive period.

The Ba' is a cork-filled leather ball, displayed in certain Kirkwall shop windows before the day of the game. The event has no time limit, or restriction on numbers of players, and begins on the Kirk Green in front of the cathedral, where the two 'towns' meet, and the ball is thrown up to commence the diversion. The teams are immediately intent on taking the ball – by hand, foot and scuffle – into their opponents' territory, and ultimately their 'goal', aided by members of the assembled crowd should extra force be needed. For the Uppies their goal is 'MacKinson's Corner' (where Main Street meets Junction Road), and for the Doonies the target area is the water along Kirkwall's sea front (the ball must touch the water). The ball is usually presented at the end of the proceedings to the player popularly acclaimed – usually after much altercation – as the worthiest competitor.

How the game originated is uncertain, but some say it evolved from a tussle or sporting rivalry between the Viking Jarl's men and the attendants of the bishop of this once Scandinavian diocese.

5 JANUARY

Auld Yule

This tradition was the equivalent of the English Twelfth Night, and was the beginning of the Feast of Epiphany the next day. A time of great merrymaking and games with tastes of the day to come . . .

6 JANUARY

Uphalieday

The Feast of Epiphany in the medieval calendar was called 'Uphalieday' in Scotland and was the end of the Twelve Days of Christmas or the Daft Days. It is remembered for us by *Adam King's Calendar* (1588): 'When Christ was revealed first to the gentiles be the starre whilk guydit the thre kingis to Bethleem.' Tradition tells how the three kings brought gifts to the infant Jesus: Melchior, gold (symbol of royalty); Caspar, frankincense (symbol of divinity); and Balthazar, myrrh (symbol of the sorrows to come). The leader of the household revels would be the one who found a bean in their piece of the Uphalieday Cake – thus they were Queen (or King) Bean.

Customs varied on this day throughout Scotland. In the Borders, for instance, they favoured the baking of a cake into which was placed a coin for luck (the recipient of the coin was the lucky one), while elsewhere they favoured each member of the family burning evergreen leaves on the living-room fire to bring good luck to the home for a year. At court, masques and burlesques were enacted, or productions of Lyon King of Arms Sir David Lyndsay's (*circa* 1486–1555) morality play *The Satire of the Three Estates*. For others it was a time to enjoy 'Snapdragons' – the pulling of raisins from a bowl alight with brandy; as each raisin was eaten a wish was made for granting within twelve months.

Scalloway Fire Festival, Shetland
Set some six and a half miles from Lerwick, Scalloway is the ancient capital of the islands, and holds its own *Up-Helly-Aa* on this day.

FIRST MONDAY OF THE NEW YEAR

Auld Handsel Monday
At one time in Scotland Handsel Monday was the first day of the year, but when the calendar of Pope Gregory XIII was introduced in 1752 an adjustment of eleven days took place. Many Scots resented this so they held their New Year on the first Monday after 12 January as calculated from the Julian Calendar they had been brought up with. And until almost the end of Victoria's reign it was the annual holiday of agriculture, industrial and domestic service workers.

The special flavour of the holiday is taken from its name: *handsel* is the old Scots word for a gift or tip, so it was the day upon which the lairds, ministers, farms and general employers gave treats to the poor folk of the neighbourhood as well as their own employees. In many parts of Scotland the handsel was in the form of a substantial breakfast and the menu would include the delicacy *powsowdie* (sheep's head broth), beefsteak pie and plum duff, all washed down with local ale or whisky.

The actual celebrations took place just after midnight on Auld Handsel Day, with a round of first-footing, horn blowing, dancing and processional visiting. Games, races and cockfighting were general but certain places had their own events: at Callander they favoured practical jokes, while at Currie it was rifle shooting; at Kirkcaldy they had a range of athletics at Ravenscraig Castle and at Wemyss they visited the caves. It all depended on the local people; they used to say that Auld Handsel Day at Auchterderran was douce, but jolly at Dunfermline. In some places gambling was favoured, with raffles for household commodities and dicing for small stakes. In the country towns Auld

Handsel Monday was treated as a market day, with the main attractions being street stalls selling treacle pieces (sandwiches of syrup), sweets like 'conversation lozenges', gingerbread and fruit.

The day after the festivities was called Roking-Day, because the roks, or spinning wheels, were uncovered again and work recommenced. As the old song said:

> Yule's come an' Yule's gane, an' we ha'e
>   feasted weel,
> Sae Jock maun to his flail again, an'
>   Jenny tae her wheel.

The local Kirk Sessions were very much against Auld Handsel Monday for they believed it encouraged the poor to disorderly behaviour; special sessions at Aberdour were held, for instance, to admonish the tiddly parishioners. There were pockets of resistance to its cancellation, particularly in Dunfermline where the Handsel holiday lasted a week; it was finally abolished in that town in 1870.

11 JANUARY

The Burning of the Clavie

The fishing village of Burghead, which sits on the eastern horn of Burghead Bay, Moray Firth, has a legendary antiquity; so much so that it has been identified with the second-century cartographer Ptolomey, of Alexandria's *Alata Castra*. It is of fitting oldness, then, to witness each year the Burning of the Clavie, undoubtedly the most celebrated of the remnants of the fire festivals of Yule which use to blaze ceremonially on Scotland's northern and eastern coasts.

The ritual is said to derive its name from the Gaelic *cliabh*, meaning a basket. According to the locals the ceremony goes back to the days of the Druids, and also has some relationship with the Norse traditions of fire-worship. The relics of these rituals lived long in these parts and developed by the seventeenth century into a 'cleansing rite' by which the townsfolk, by making circuits of the harbour bearing flaming fir-torches, expunged the evil eye from the fishing boats for a year.

Food and drink were also carried to the boats in the harbour, an obvious remnant of votive offerings to the gods of the sea.

The *dramatis personae* of the event today are still the Clavie King and his helpers. The Clavie itself is traditionally made from a tar barrel (or its modern equivalent) sawn in half, the staves of a herring cask, and an eight-foot-long salmon-fisherman's pole called a 'spoke'. The half barrel is fixed to the spoke with a specially forged nail and hammered home with a stone. Traditionally no iron must be used in this process, suggesting a link with the primitive magic of this area still rich with Pictish artifacts. The barrel is then filled with tar and combustibles, while the herring staves secure the Clavie to the spoke, and provide a cage for a carrier to get his head through.

Burning peat is placed in the Clavie by the Clavie King, and the flaming bundle is carried round the streets of the old town by a relay of men before being taken to the top of a knoll called the Doorie, once a supposed centre of Pictish fire-worship. In 1809 a freestone pillar was erected on the knoll by a local laird to receive the Clavie, and today it is referred to as the Clavie Stone. There more fuel is heaped on and finally the blazing embers are scattered down the hillside where people scramble for the glowing cinders. Each ember is said to bring good luck for the rest of the year as a charm against evil spirits. Once this was the job of children who ran round the streets throwing embers through open doorways with the salutation 'Here's yer clavie!'

25 JANUARY

Honouring the National Bard

The poet Robert Burns has become the central figure of a vague Scottish 'religion', a custom of good-fellowship and inebriated conviviality to celebrate the brotherhood of man. Around his birthdate Burns is honoured from Melbourne, Australia, to Grangemouth, Scotland, by Christian and atheist, Nationalist and Communist, extremist and liberal, Jacobite and Hanoverian, all of whom see the poet as the personification of their own thoughts.

For those who know little about Robert Burns, and there have been hundreds of biographies written about him, suffice it to say that he was born at Alloway near Ayr, on 25 January 1759 in a cottage built by his father, a tenant farmer and horticulturist from Kincardineshire. Burns was better educated than most of his class of the day, and although toiling hard in the fields found time to write poetry, of which the anthology *Poems Chiefly in the Scottish Dialect*, published in 1786, ultimately made him world famous. Burns rebelled against the oppressive nature of the Presbyterian Church of his day, and his literary caricatures of religious hypocrisy and cant have found fellow-feeling amongst the Scots every since. He died on 21 July 1796.

To remember his sociability nine of Burns's friends in life gathered together on 29 January 1801 (his biographer James Currie had mistaken the date of the poet's birthday), at his 'auld clay biggin'' in Alloway, and held the first 'Burns Supper'; and thereafter they met annually. Even so it was not until 1809 that these friends referred to themselves as a 'Burns Club' and were pipped at the post by Greenock devotees who held their inaugural meeting as a club on 21 July 1801. It was not until the centenary of his birth in 1859 that the idea of an annual birthday celebration caught on nationwide.

Over the years the format of a Burns Supper has developed, and today it usually falls into three main parts: the Supper; the Speeches; the Songs. The Supper, usually described on a menu in the Lowland tongue, is festive fair for homely folk. Usually each dish is set out with a motto or rhymed tribute to its character. The first course might be Scotch broth, or the chicken soup known as cock-a-leekie, with the sentiment:

> God bless your Honours a' your days,
> Wi sowps o' kail an' brats o' claes.

The haggis, in honour of which Burns wrote 'Address to the Haggis' in 1786, and said to have been composed extempore at dinner at the house of the merchant Andrew Bruce, Castlehill, Edinburgh, has place of honour on the table. It is piped in and 'addressed' with a recitation of Burns's lines, which begin:

> Fair fa' your honest, sonsie face,
> Great Chieftain o' the Puddin-race!
> Aboon them a' ye tak your place,
>   Painch, tripe, or thairm:
> Weel are ye worthy of a grace
>   As lang's my airm.

Thereafter the haggis is solemnly cut and eaten. The whole meal is preceded by a grace traditionally accredited to Burns, as in the collection of James Grierson of Dalgoner, and said to have been uttered by the poet at the table of the Earl of Selkirk while Burns toured Galloway in July 1793:

> Some hae meat and canna eat,
> And some wad eat that want it;
> But we hae meat, and we can eat,
> And sae the Lord be thanket.

The main speeches and toasts include the loyal toast, to the head of state of whichever country the supper is being held in, the 'Immortal Memory' of Burns himself, the guests and the lassies, the latter often being proposed with chauvinist wit although with a mollifying conclusion such as:

> Eve's bonnie squad priests wyte them
>   sheerly,
> For our grand fa'
> But still, but still I like them dearly,
> God bless them a'!

Afterwards the company listens to songs associated with Burns's own collections of traditional rhymes and the proceedings are concluded with the singing of 'Auld Lang Syne' in Burns's reworking. The supper breaks up in happy contentment mirroring Burns's own words:

> It's no in titles nor in rank,
> It's no in wealth like Lon'on Bank,
> To purchase peace and rest;
> If happiness hae not her seat
>   and centre in the breast,
> We may be wise or rich or great
>   but never can be blest.

31 JANUARY

Up-Helly-Aa, Lerwick, Shetland

Lying at a latitude of sixty degrees north, and 180 miles west of Bergen, Norway, and the same distance north of Aberdeen, the hundred-island Shetlands, the *Ultima Thule* of the Romans, cherish their links with the Vikings. And the *Up-Helly-Aa* events at Lerwick (and at Scalloway, Nesting and Girlsta, and Brae on different dates) celebrate the end of Yule – the old feast of the Twenty-Fourth Night – and are probably the most spectacular and emotive fire festivals in Europe. *Helly* is the modern Norse *Hellig* (holy), and *Up-Helly-Aa* means 'end of the holy days'.

Up to the late 1880s the Shetland Fire Festival at Lerwick consisted of local men and youths making sport by dragging blazing tar barrels through the streets. By 1889 a Norse longship had replaced the tar barrel, and the whole company had taken on a boisterous aspect with an accompaniment of horn blowing while guisers (mummers in disguises) visited houses for good luck.

Today's celebrations are modern in historical terms – Lerwick as a town and parish only dates from 1700 – but the origins are likely to stem from memories of the Norse occupation when the cadavers of kings and chiefs were sent to Valhalla (the Viking heaven) in fiery splendour. Wrapped in furs, and with weapons lying alongside, the corpses of the leaders were placed in longships which were set on fire and left to drift on the tide. Nowadays this act is remembered in a thirty-one-foot model of a Viking ship, complete with heraldic shields and dragon figurehead. Once these ships, rowed by thirty-two oarsmen, made sporadic raids on the northern islands and coastline, bringing Viking hordes to scavenge and pillage. With shield, helmet and chainmail, sword, javelin and battleaxe these Vikings outmatched the primitive weapons of the Picts of the north. Hereabouts the Vikings in their dragon boats held sway from AD 874 to the fifteenth century, and the spirit of such chiefs as Harald Haarfagre (Harold the Fairhead), once a visitor to Shetland, is remembered in *Up-Helly-Aa*.

The mock Viking ship is paraded through Lerwick by the principal of the revels, the Chief Guiser, or the Guiser Jarl, and his 500 henchmen dressed in Viking costume. The Jarls, by the by, were the governors whom King Harold Haarfagre put in place to collect the taxes he levied for his central government. As darkness descends, the longship is set at the head of a great torchlight procession, while the musicians play the 'Galley Song'. At the appropriate time the crowds will sing 'The Norseman's Home', and the ship is fired by throwing lighted torches into it. The vessel takes about an hour to burn. The parade then re-forms and parties continue until the early hours of the morning.

2

The Rites of Springtime

In spring, the first season of the year, which astronomically begins in the northern hemisphere at the vernal equinox (around 21 March) and ends with the summer solstice, the folk of the northlands sought to cleanse their surroundings of evil. In the abbeys the novices played a game of football, kicking a ball around the abbey precincts to gather on it the year's evils. Symbolically the ball was then kicked through the abbey gate, thereby removing twelve months' evil. After the Reformation such football games were carried on by the menfolk of Scotland from Scone to Duns. At Jedburgh a more sinister reasons haunts their ball game.

EARLY FEBRUARY

Jedburgh's Hand Ba'

Traditionally the Border town of Jedburgh, one of the oldest Border burghs with its now ruined Augustinian abbey, first founded as a priory in *circa* 1138 by King David I, had two ball games. The Callants' Ba' game, at Candlemas, and the Men's Ba' game at Fastern's E'en. The first of the Scottish quarter-days — when bills were paid and servants hired — Candlemas, appears on the ecclesiastical calendar on 2 February, and is a feast in honour of the purification of the Blessed Virgin (it was once a custom in Scotland for pupils to give gifts to teachers on this day). Fastern's E'en is the movable feast of Shrove Tuesday known as Bannoch Nicht in Scotland when oatmeal bannocks were baked. Today the Fastern's E'en Ba' game predominates and takes place between two teams, the Uppies and the Doonies, the former being those born above the site of Jedburgh's old mercat cross, and the latter those born to the downward end of the town; thus the Uppies play towards Castlehill and the Doonies towards Townfoot.

Beginning at two o'clock, the game commences with a ball, decorated with streaming coloured ribbons, being thrown up above the town's market place. The game has no written rules or referee and is basically handball with the ball being jockeyed around the town. No game will be deemed worthwhile unless the ball ends up in the River Jed with the players splashing after it. The Fastern's E'en Ba' is followed by a dinner given by the Jethart Callants' Club who organize the game.

The origins of the game are disputed, some saying that it commemorates a battle between the Scots and the English at nearby Ferniehirst Castle. Here the Scots, legend has it, hacked off the heads of their enemies to kick them like footballs through the streets (i.e., the modern folk relic being the balls with streamers). In reality, though, the game is probably much older.

In 1849, the Rev A.P. Syme of Lilliesleaf recalled, the Jedburgh ball game fell foul of the town magistrates who wanted to have it stopped because it was too boisterous. The townsfolk challenged the magistrates' position at the High Court at Edinburgh, which ruled that the magistrates had no legal right to ban the game; incidentally a similar game was stopped at Melrose for the same reason in the 1890s.

10 FEBRUARY

Up-Helly-Aa, Nesting and Girlsta, Shetland

14 FEBRUARY

St Valentine's Day

The festival of love and lovers, derived from the Roman *Lupercalia* – feasting the shepherd god Pan and Juno Februalis – took its name from the priest and martyr Valentine who was beheaded in the year 270 by the Roman Emperor Claudius II. In Roman times the eligible young men and women wrote their individual names on separate pieces of paper and placed them in two boxes, one for each sex. As the names were alternately drawn, each was the other's *amator* for the ensuing year.

It seems that a similar custom was widespread in Scotland. In 1774 the naturalist and traveller Thomas Pennant (1726–98) wrote in his *Tours in Scotland* how 'young people draw Valentines and from them collect their fortune in the nuptial state'. The custom was certainly popular in Robert Burns's day for he mentions the practice in his 1788 poem 'Tam Glen':

> Yestreen at the Valentine's dealing,
> My hert to my mou' gied a sten;
> > *My heart was in my mouth*
> For thrice I drew ane without failing,
> And thrice it was written, Tam Glen.

When the slips were drawn the young people exchanged gifts, and from this developed the custom of giving letters and valentine cards, many of which were to quote the love poems of Robert Burns.

Sir Walter Scott mentions another Scottish custom in his *The Fair Maid of Perth*, which he subtitled *St Valentine's Day*: 'Tomorrow is St Valentine's Day, when every bird chooses his mate. I will plague you no longer now, providing you will let me see you from your window tomorrow when the sun first peeps over the eastern hill, and give me right to be your Valentine for the year.'

MID FEBRUARY

St Andrews Festival
This festival of art, music, poetry, drama, cabaret, films and exhibitions was started in 1971, the idea of two university students. From the start the festival achieved great popularity and it was decided to continue it biennially, so festivals are planned for 1991 and every two years thereafter. Organized by the Festival Society from 1975, the festival forms an important link between town and gown involving such bodies as the students' Kate Kennedy Club (see page 31) and the town's celebrated Byre Theatre.

1 MARCH

Whuppity Scoorie, Lanark

The name of this pleasingly odd custom is a local corruption of 'Whuppity Scoorze' and is also called 'Whuppity Stoorie', the traditional name for a bad fairy in many parts of Scotland. Once played by the youth of Lanark, it developed as a children's event, starting off from the cross by the old parish church.

Each child was given, or made, a tightly rolled ball of paper to which was attached a piece of string some two feet long. When the church bells pealed six o'clock the children then rushed three times round the church striking each other with the paper balls now being swung round the head. The balls are a more modern replacement for rolled up caps or 'bunnets'.

The custom is undated in origin – and its name was only first used publicly in the *Hamilton Advertiser* in 1893 – but it is likely, say some local historians, to come from a superstition concerning the chasing away of devils who were deemed to lurk in the 'whirls of stoor' (March dust) to work evil in the fields. The basic intention was to beat out the devil from the fields and ensure a bounteous harvest. The ringing of the church bells (at the time of Compline, the last service of the day in the medieval church) obviously mirrors the pagan clashing of metal to frighten the devils away, as the thirteenth-century theologian Durandus wrote: 'Bells are rung in processions that devils may flee.' From the mid-nineteenth century the church bell was pealed at six o'clock at Lanark for the next six months after Whuppity Scoorie, and then was silent for six months.

So the custom has all the associations of a pagan feast, including the three-times circle of the church, in mimic of the Druidic three times round the sacred grove for luck. Yet there are others who point to an eighteenth-century origin. Indeed, in the nineteenth century Whuppity Scoorie was a more violent affair: the Lanark lads would march to nearby New Lanark to fight with the youths of that eighteenth-century planned industrial village, first set out by the Glasgow manufacturer and banker David Dale in 1785. Stone-throwing became a part of Whuppity Scoorie and had to be discouraged. As the youths ran from the police, the Rev A.D. Robertson noted in his *Lanark* (1974), they would chant:

> Hurrah boys, Hurrah.
> We have won the day,
> We've beat Sergeant Sutherland,
> And chased his men away.

With the alternative lines:

> We've met the bold New Lanark boys
> And chased them doon the brae!

The fighting was officially banned by the Lanark magistrates before the Second World War. Thus some historians believe that Whuppity Scoorie actually began with the Lanark/New Lanark conflict and is no older than the social reformer Robert Owen's (1771–1858) development of his father-in-law's (David Dale) village.

17 MARCH

Up-Helly-Aa, Brae, Shetland

Spring also sees the beginning of the burgeoning folk, music and song festivals, which go on until November, the first being the Folk Festival at Inverness (third week of March). The rest may be summarized thus:

Edinburgh Folk Festival (around 6–15 April). Folk-music played in pubs around Edinburgh.
Glenfarg Folk Festival (around 14–16 April). Concerts; ceilidh; children's songs and drama.
Shetland Folk Festival (around 27–30 April). Concerts and dances throughout the islands.
Girvan (around 28–30 April). Family–based folk festival based on traditional music and song.
Glencoe and Lochleven Music Festival (around 12–14 May). Some sixty events covering Cajun to ceilidh.
Banchory Festival of Scottish Music (around 13 May). A one–day competitive event which is run by the

Banchory Strathspey and Reel Society, which means fiddle, accordion and piano competitions.

Buchan Heritage Festival (around 19–20 May). All types of music, competition and also those for ballads, poetry and Doric verse.

Orkney Folk Festival of Traditional Music (around 25–28 May). Purely a festival of traditional music with supper dances and ceilidhs for all in parishes and islands.

Islay Festival/Féis Ile (around 26–27 May/2–3 June/9–10 June). A community festival of Gaelic and English song at concerts, ceilidhs and dances throughout Islay.

Isle of Arran Festival of Folk (around 5–11 June). Wide range of music and song from all over Scotland.

Keith Traditional Music Festival (around 9–11 June). Ceilidhs, concerts, informal music sessions.

Highland Traditional Music Festival (around 23–25 June). Main events in the National Hotel, Dingwall.

Blairgowrie Folk and Blues Festival (around 30 June–2 July).

Newcastleton Traditional Music Festival (around 30 June–2 July). Full range of events to include competitions for mouth organ, tin whistle and poetry.

Glasgow Folk Festival (around 3–9 July). Begun 1979 to promote international folk with an emphasis on dance.

Dundee Folk Festival (around 12–15 July). Dubbed a 'celebration of traditional music'.

Stonehaven Folk Festival (around 21–23 July).

Upper Donside Ceilidh Club (around 22 July).

Rhinns of Islay Celtic Festival (around 28 July–5 August). A Pan–Celtic festival.

Auchtermuchty Festival (around 11–13 August). The music festival is part of a ten–day community festival.

Kirriemuir Traditional Music Festival (around 1–3 September). Begun in 1965, the festival is one of traditional Scottish music.

Tarbert Music Festival (around 15–17 September). Begun 1988 with a wide range of traditional and contemporary folk music.

Penicuik Folk Festival (around 13–15 October). Concerts for adults and children.

Aberdeen Traditional Arts Weekend (around 13–15 October). Concerts and workshops forming part of Aberdeen's 'Alternative Festival'.

Glasgow Tryst (around 24 November–2 December). Bylined a 'celebration of Scottish music' and set largely within the Merchant City.

3

April Fools and Beltane Fires

1 APRIL

Hunt the Gowk

With New Year's Day once celebrated in Scotland on 25 March, the first of April closed the octave of days at the end of the vernal equinox, and became an excuse for a day of foolery. The old season structure remained as a race memory into the Middle Ages and probably Scotland's 'Hunting the Gowk' (*La'na cubhag* in Gaelic), the equivalent of England's All Fools Day, developed in its later form with a boost from French influence.

The French have an equivalent custom called *poisson d'Avril* ('Fish of April') and it is likely that the foolery Scotland was to take up came in the baggage train of Mary Queen of Scots on her return from exile in France in 1561. 'Gowk' has two meanings in Scotland, 'fool' and 'cuckoo', the latter being a bird associated with foolishness.

Writing in his *The Book of Days* (1869), Robert Chambers reminds us of the Scottish custom once enacted on this day:

> In the northern part of the island, they are not content to make a neighbour believe some single piece of absurdity. There, the object being, we shall say, to befool simple Andrew Thomson, Wag No 1 sent him away with a letter to a friend two miles off, professedly asking for some useful information, or requesting a loan of some article, but in reality containing only the words:
>
> > This is the first day of April,
> > Hunt the gowk another mile.
>
> Wag No 2, catching up the idea of his correspondent, tells Andrew with a grave face that it is not in

his power, &c; but if he will go with another note to such a person, he will get what is wanted. Off Andrew trudges with this second note to Wag No 3, who treats him in the same manner; and so on he goes, till some one of the series, taking pity on him, hints the trick that has been practised upon him. A successful affair of this kind will keep rustic society in merriment for a week . . .

The timescale in which one could make a fool of any-one was from dawn to midday. Thereafter if tricks were tried the children would chant to their persecutor:

> The Day of the Gowk is gane,
> You're the gowk and I'm nane.

A SCOTTISH EASTER

Coincidentally the pagan festival of the spring equi-nox corresponds with Christian Easter. As the season of rebirth, Easter was celebrated in pagan times in Scotland as the feast of Frigga (the Teutonic mother goddess) in the territory where Scandinavian influences held sway. In time, as the Celtic Church gave way to the Roman, Easter was called *Pasch* or *Pesse* in Scotland, a name linked with the greatest of all symbols of birth, the egg. So 'pace egg' became an important Easter custom in Scotland.

Undoubtedly, in Scotland eggs were substituted for the human sacrifices of heathendom, as a symbol of fertility, purity and resurrection, and the custom of rolling eggs was a descendant of the pagan egg dances. It was (and is) mostly children who roll eggs on the Saturday afternoon of Easter. These eggs were coloured with natural dyes – whin blossom produced yellow, and logwood or beetroot gave purple. There were many superstitions, of course, associated with eggs in Scotland. For instance the first egg a hen laid was kept as a lucky talisman, and the empty shells of rolled eggs were always smashed to pieces lest witches use the remaining halves as vehicles to fly through the air. Concerning the pace egg custom D.A. Mackenzie wrote this in 1917: 'I used to roll dyed eggs on "Egg

Monday" when I was a boy in Ross and Cromarty, and we had an "Egg Sunday". We afterwards burned whin and searched for shellfish. In Edinburgh here, I find the dyed eggs are rolled in Bruntsfield Links. The custom was quite common all over Scotland until recently. It has been stamped out by unimaginative school-teachers and parsons.'

Hot cross buns, eaten mainly on Good Friday, are the Christian symbols of the heathen buns baked to represent the full moon. The Scottish equivalent are more spicy than other varieties. In the far north they also included a breakfast meal of pesse pie (a dish of wildfowl) dressed in the feathers of the bird used, to celebrate Easter Day Morn, where the sun represented the risen Saviour (cf. the pagan sun dances).

The pace egg and hot cross bun traditions are still enacted in Scotland, but the ritual use of other foods at Easter only remains in folk memory. On Car Sunday, (the fifth Sunday in Lent), for instance, a platter of peas was always included in the family meal – a bundle of peas was burned and the resultant roasted peas were tossed in butter (or in later times steeped peas were used). Easter peas were usually given to visitors calling after church, peas being the old sacramental gift.

Up to the Reformation Palm Sunday processions were common (wherein boughs were carried to represent those strewn before Christ on his entry into

Jerusalem). They lasted longest as a tradition at Lanark (where it involved grammar-school boys) and in the parishes of Speyside.

EARLY APRIL

Kate Kennedy Procession, St Andrews
This colourful costume pageant of the University of St Andrews is thought to have originated *circa* 1848 as an end-of-term romp by fourth-year students attending the natural philosophy class; records show that this class 'wore a variety from ordinary dress'. Founded in 1411 by Bishop Henry Wardlaw, the university developed into three colleges by the mid-sixteenth century, namely St Salvator's (1450), St Leonard's (1512) and St Mary's (1537). St Salvator's is the starting point of the pageant today. Founded by Bishop James Kennedy, St Salvator's College quad is the assembly area for the procession headed by 'Kate Kennedy' its central character, who tradition makes one of the daughters of Bishop Kennedy's brother, Gilbert Kennedy, Lord Kennedy of Dunure, and his wife Catherine Maxwell. It is also said that young Kate was the chatelaine of her uncle's household. How Kate came to be associated with the pageant is now obscure, but some have ascribed her procession to a relic of a local festival celebrating the coming of spring, or indeed the founding of the college.

Charles Rogers, writing in *Scotland Social and Domestic* (1869), compares Kate Kennedy with 'the miracle plays of the Romish Church'. In his day, Kate Kennedy was on horseback. 'Each member of the procession,' wrote Rogers, 'represents some historical character. The Pope is seldom absent. The more popular of the Stuart kings are represented. Roman citizens and Greek philosophers are occasionally present. The Irish peasant, talking blarney, and the St Andrews fishwoman, with her creel, are conspicuous.' Rogers mixes the 'origins' of the celebration with 'honours paid in Romish times to the memory of St Catherine', the 'good services' of Bishop James Kennedy and his supposed dedication of the college bell to St Catherine (her feast being 25 November).

In truth it is likely to be none of these and nothing more than an early Victorian excuse for student mummery at which *circa* 1848 event a student dressed as 'Kate' and capered at the centre of a noisy frolic which was to spill out on to the streets of St Andrews. When the romp became too boisterous, and an excuse to pillory town and gown personalities in its dumb show, the university authorities tried to ban it, and its suppression made it a symbol of student freedom.

By the 1860s the Kate Kennedy Pageant had become a procession through the main streets of St Andrews and on one outrageous day in 1874 the students came into conflict with the burgh authorities and the whole thing was banned. And this ban remained total, except for a procession on 5 March 1881, until 1926.

For his address to the university of 3 May 1922, the new Rector, Sir James Matthew Barrie, took 'courage' as his theme and this was to inspire two students. During the address Barrie mused on the supposition as to the historical figures associated with the university that he would like to have met and walked with. The two students, Donald Kennedy and James Doak, saw the revival of the Kate Kennedy procession as the nearest thing to Barrie's idea. So today some hundred or so characters associated with the university and Scotland's story parade through the streets. The sequence of the parade is as follows with the main 'section leaders':

Prelude: Led by St Andrew

The early Church: Preceded by St Regulus, or St Rule, the fabled bringer of St Andrew's bones to the cathedral site

The War of Independence: Bishop William de Lamberton (*circa* 1265–1328) who consecrated the cathedral in 1318

The founding of the university: Bishop Henry Wardlaw (*circa* 1372–1440), the founder of the university

The Master of St John's College: Laurence of Lindores (*circa* 1373–1437), first Rector of the university

The founders of St Leonard's College: Archbishop Alexander Stewart (1495–1513), co-founder with Prior John Hepburn (*circa* 1460–1522)

Scottish poets: William Dunbar (*circa* 1460–*circa* 1530) leads the group

Martyrs of the Kirk: Patrick Hamilton (*circa* 1504–28), burned for his faith before the gateway of St Salvator's

The founders of St Mary's College: Archbishop James Beaton (*circa* 1473–1539)

The Reformation: John Knox (1507–72)

Crown and courtiers: Mary Queen of Scots (1542–87) who visited the town many times

Early scientists: John Napier of Merchiston (1550–1617), mathematician

The National Covenant: Alexander Henderson (1583–1645)

The '15 and the '45: William Murray, Marquess of Tullibardine (1689–1746)

Revolution and reform: George Dempster of Dunnichen (1732–1818)

Eighteenth-century scholarship: Robert Fergusson (1750–74)

Nineteenth-century citizens: Sir Hugh Lyon Playfair (1786–1861)

Nineteenth-century students: John Honey (*circa* 1781–1814)

The founder of the University of Dundee: Mary Ann Baxter of Balgavies (1801–84)

Figures of recent times: John, third Marquess of Bute (1847–1900)

The equipage of the Lady Katherine Kennedy

Traditionally Kate Kennedy is played by a 'beardless bejant', that is a male first-year student, and 'she' rides in a carriage in the procession with her uncle the bishop, dressed in his full canonical rig-out. The procession emerges from the wooden gates of St Salvator's quad at 2 p.m. and proceeds down North Street to the castle, via the Scores, and then, by way of Market Street and the cathedral, returns to the quad.

These days the pageant is one of the most vibrant and colourful in Europe. The stated aims of the fifty-plus all-male Kate Kennedy Club are: to foster the good relations between town and gown; to raise money for charities; to foster the traditions of the university like the Silver Arrow archery competition, the May morning swim, maypole and bonfire and the Kate Kennedy Ball (not to be invited is to die socially!).

Two other St Andrews University customs are worthy of note:

Meal Monday (February)

No classes in the university. In medieval times the more poverty-stricken of the students went home to collect their mid-term rations of oatmeal on this day.

Raisin Monday/Weekend (early November)

Traditionally the first-year students at St Andrews University are called bejants and bejantines (i.e. from the French term *bec-jaune*, 'yellow beak' or fledgling), and they are required by custom to acquire a 'Senior Man' or 'Senior Woman' student (usually third or fourth year) as their mentor during the first year. These students are called their 'academic parents' and help to introduce the fledglings into university society and university life.

On Raisin Monday, during the Martinmas Term, it is customary for the bejants and bejantines to give their academic parents a pound of raisins as a gift in exchange for a ribald receipt in Latin; these days it is usual for the gift to be a bottle of wine. Traditionally too, the bejants and bejantines are expected to dress in outrageous 'theme' costumes to receive their receipts and they gather in the quad of St Salvator's College where, in recent years, large quantities of shaving cream are squirted on all and sundry.

16 APRIL (NEAREST SATURDAY TO)

Culloden Memorial Service

Culloden Moor, some six miles east-north-east of Inverness, has always been an emotive place to where, from time immemorial, people trekked on pilgrimage to drink the waters of the *Tobar n'Oige* (the Well of Youth). In more modern times it was called the 'Cloutie Well', for folk would tie 'clouts' (cloths/rags) on to the surrounding vegetation to seal the wish they had wished at the well.

Since the 1920s, and maybe sporadically before, folk have gathered at Culloden Moor — Drummossie Moor to the Highlanders — to remember the sleety, cold morning of 16 April 1746, whereupon was enacted the last full-scale battle ever to take place on British soil. The

Battle of Culloden was the climax of the Jacobite rising of 1745, known as the Rebellion of the '45, during the reign of George II. Charles Edward Stuart had landed in Scotland bent on restoring his father, James Francis Edward Stuart, to the throne of Great Britain instead of the Hanoverian succession and had marched with his army as far as Derby to try to seize London. But, disappointed with the lack of English support, Charles retreated north. Meanwhile, his cousin William Augustus, Duke of Cumberland, marched towards him with a strong counter force. They met at Culloden and Charles's army was massacred.

The memorial service to commemorate this dark day is held at the cairn on Culloden Battlefield.

MID-APRIL

The Links Market, Kirkcaldy

Records show that this market began with an Easter Chartered Fair in 1305, and it is still claimed to be the largest street fair in the world. The market is held on the sea-front esplanade, built 1922–3, and the streets around the Bethelfield area are clogged with crowds drawn to the showmen's carousels and the street barkers' stalls. Illumination has always been a feature of the fair, which is an impressive sight even from the south side of the Firth of Forth.

1 MAY

Beltane and Mayday

Beltane was one of the principal festivals of the Celtic year. It celebrated the renewal of vegetation and marked the time when the cattle were driven out of their winter quarters to crop the new grass. It survived as one of the old quarter-days of Scotland (15 May) and entered the pre-Reformation calendar as the Feast of the Finding of the Holy Cross (3 May); the latter day was called 'Rood Day' in Scotland and it celebrated the legendary discovery of the cross on which Christ was crucified, by the Empress Helena, the mother of Constantine the Great. In many parts of Scotland people would take fragments of the Beltane bannock (*bannach Bealltain)* as their Holy Communion.

In the days of Celtic heathendom, of course, Beltane was celebrated with bonfires and the devout were cautioned only to collect certain woods for the fires for good luck. The *Carmina Gadelica* reminds us of the poem concerning the wood collection:

> Choose the willow of the streams,
> Choose the hazel of the rocks,
> Choose the alder of the marshes,
> Choose the birch of the waterfalls.
> Choose the ash of the shade,
> Choose the elm of the brae,
> Choose the oak of the sun.

In some places annual pilgrimages to holy places, like wells and shrines, were begun on Beltane Day. And all over Scotland young girls would get up before dawn to collect the dew, as washing one's face with this was said to produce a clear complexion, and to enhance beauty. This custom derived from Celtic times, when on May morning the shamans collected dew water for use in their rituals.

Certain localities became associated with Beltane fires – Arthur's Seat, Edinburgh, Kinnoul Hill, Perthshire and Dechmont Hill, Cambuslang for example – and several locations in Scotland took their names from the Beltane rituals: *Tulach Bealltuinn* (Beltane Hill) became Tullybelton, Perthshire; *Teinteach* (place of fire), Tinto, near Lanark; and *Tor-Bealltuinn* (Beltane hillock), Tarbolton, Ayrshire.

The maypole in Scotland was the survival of the ritual collecting of rowan, birch and other woods for devotion of the spirits of vegetation, and is phallic in symbolism. Dancing and games took place at Maytime and several places elected and crowned a 'queen' to grace the activities.

FOURTH WEEK OF MAY

Atholl Highland Parade/Atholl Highland Gathering

Today the Atholl Highlanders remain the last private

army in Europe. The regiment was raised as part of the British army to fight in the American War of Independence in 1777, but was disbanded three years later. It was re-formed in 1839 by Lord Glenlyon and acted as bodyguard to Queen Victoria during her stay at Blair Castle in 1844. The regiment is the sole survivor of the ancient custom whereby the King of Scotland had no army but relied on local chiefs to bring their clan forces to support him in time of war. Today the Highlanders are present at the Atholl Parade and the Atholl Gathering at Blair Atholl, Perthshire.

The Atholl Highland meetings are formed, as the *Perthshire Courier* recorded in 1827, 'for the purpose of preserving some of the best traits of the ancient character and spirit of their countrymen in the district'. It was named 'The Atholl Gathering' in 1841.

LAST WEEK OF MAY, FIRST WEEK OF JUNE

Clackmannan District Arts Festival

Started in 1986, it offers music, circus, a real-ale festival, puppets, drama and art, and a family fun day at Cochrane Park, Alloa. Poetry and folk festivities are also on offer.

MOST OF MAY

Mayfest, Citywide, Glasgow

A product of the late 1980s, this festival has expanded rapidly. Its organizers describe it thus:

Mayfest is recognized as one of Europe's key festivals for theatre, dance, music and related performing arts. But, while international in policy and style, its foundations are Scottish and it provides a platform for the best in contemporary Scottish culture. Like many major festivals, the Mayfest programme is confirmed at a late stage. You'll be able to pick up a full programme in March. But once again we are sure to see interesting and surprising productions from all over the world. There will also be an outstanding cabaret, music and entertainment programme. And dozens of performances will tour to, and arise from Glasgow's communities.

The whole tone of Mayfest is an exaltation of proletariat culture, from local experimental theatre to the drama of Leningrad's theatre companies, and from nationalistic Celtic melodies to the music of Soviet Georgia.

4

Riding the Bounds
and Marches

JUNE TO MID-AUGUST

The Borders common ridings are for some the highlight
of all Scottish traditions and festivals, with a spirit that is
unique. Each of the Border towns that hold these annual
celebrations have their own local peculiarities but the
format is typical from Langholm to Duns.

In Borderland parlance the term 'Borders' usually
means the Scottish side of the Border line, while the
'English side' is thought of as the 'Border Country'. In
political terms these lands were called the Marches
and were administered and monitored by Scottish and
English knights under the direction of the sheriffs of
Northumberland for the English monarch and the sheriffs of Roxburgh and Berwick for the Scottish sovereign.

The theme that links today's Border common ridings is Anglo-Saxon in origin, based on the need to
ride the marches – in effect the time-honoured and
accepted boundaries between the parishes – in order to
discourage encroachment. The concept of a fixed border between England and Scotland was more appar-
ent than real up to the mid-1400s, and it was not
legally accepted until the sixteenth century. Up to
the seventeenth century the Borderland areas from
Berwick-upon-Tweed in the east and Langholm in the
west were 'debatable land'.

When the eighteenth century brought its established
enclosures, riding of the Marches became unnecessary,
but the former need to do so was reinvigorated with the
perceived romance of former days. In truth the common
ridings of some places today are mere inventions and
have no basis in historical tradition. For many people
a grain or two of genuine antiquity has been built into
the local pride and friendly rivalry of towns – be it
tongue-in-cheek seriousness on the one hand and a

black eye on the other – that is a part of Borderland character.

West Linton Festival and Saturday Rideout, beginning of June

The chief characters of this festival are the Whipman, his Lass and the Barony Herald, and the activities go back to the time in 1803 when the Whipman Benevolent Society held their annual 'Linton Play'. In those days the Whipman visited on horseback the mansions of the district and was received cordially during the morning of the festival, and the rest of the day was devoted to sporting activities. The society existed to supply mutual succour to members in times of illness and distress. The centrepiece of the festival was horsemanship, ploughmanship and horse decoration.

The Whipman Benevolent Society became extinct but the sporting aspects continued until the First World War; after the war it was revived, but the place of the horse lessened and the whole Whipman Play was revised in 1931. The whole died out during the Second World War and for some time after, to be revived in 1949.

Hawick Common Riding on first Friday and Saturday after the second Monday in June

This festival lasts over five weeks with a principal rideout and minor rideouts. The principal personages are the Cornet supported by the two previous holders of the office as the Right-Hand Man and the Left-Hand Man. The Cornet is advised by the Acting Father and his consort is the Cornet's Lass. When all the basic rideouts have taken place women take a part in the traditions with the Cornet's Lass *bussing* (dedicating anew) the burgh flag with gold and blue ribbons.

A feature of this ceremony is the honouring of the burgh boundaries and subsequent rides go to Bonchester Bridge, Lilliesleaf (twice), Roberton, Mosspaul (twice), Denholm, Teviotdale Lodge and Priesthaugh. All riders who complete the Mosspaul Rideout for the first time are given membership of the Ancient Order of Mosstroopers (the mosstroopers were the ancient Border cattle-stealers who raided for plunder over the Borderlands).

Selkirk Common Riding, Friday and Saturday after the second Monday of June

As with the other principals elsewhere the Standard Bearer of the ridings has to be 'unmarried and of good repute' and be a native of Selkirk; he is supported by four attendants. The day of the morning ride is preceded by the 'Crying the Burley' and the whole is a succession of dinners and *bussings* and flag casting. The Standard Bearer is collected from his house by a flute band and the procession begins at seven o'clock. The 'Riding of the Marches of the Royal Burgh' takes about four and a half hours. Various of the old trades and associations are represented in the parade and they have their own flags. The route is from the town, across the Ettrick Water, to Tibbie Tamson's grave, then to the Three Brethren Cairns and back by Shawburn Toll to the Market Place for the flag casting.

This common riding dates at least from the sixteenth century and tradition associates it with the disastrous battle of Flodden of 1513 when an English army under the Earl of Surrey defeated the Scots, killing King James IV and most of his nobles. It is said that of the eighty Selkirk men who went to fight at Flodden only one returned, carrying a captured English flag; the flag casting remembers this event and at the casting the poignant song 'The Flowers of the Forest' is sung.

Melrose Festival, third full week in June

Led by the Melrosian, his Right-Hand Man and Left-Hand Man (the two previous Melrosians), the festival events include showjumping and gymkhana displays (at Gibson Park) as well as the Monday evening rideout – from the Greenyards, by the Eildons, across the Tweed, up Gattonside Heights and back to Melrose via Darnick. Football matches and a fancy dress parade precede the crowning of the Festival Queen (traditionally the dux girl of Melrose Grammar School) in the grounds of Melrose Abbey.

This festival keeps tryst with the town's historic locations – the Roman fort site of Trimontium at Newstead (hailed as Scotland's oldest inhabited village and location for the oldest Masonic Lodge); the Cistercian Abbey of St Mary within the town; Abbotsford, the home of Sir Walter Scott; and Darnick Tower, a Border peel tower first built in 1425. The festival's Eildon Hill Race is now included in the British Fell Running Championships.

Peebles Riding of the Marches and Beltane Festival, middle of June

In 1621 James VI granted to Peebles the right to hold a Beltane Fair. It is held in May, and these days the proclamation of the fair has been incorporated with the Beltane Queen ceremonials. To celebrate the Diamond Jubilee of Queen Victoria in 1897 the town's burgesses resuscitated the old Riding of the March ceremonial and all of the traditions of the modern festival were drawn together.

Beltane Week begins with the installation of the Warden of the Cross Kirk with an inaugural church service; the Cornet is installed on Wednesday evening and the burgh flag is *bussed* by the Cornet's Lass. The ceremonial rideout then takes place via Neidpath Castle where the Warden of Neidpath is installed. On the Thursday the Beltane Concert takes place and the Cornet's Walk around the town. The Beltane Queen is crowned on the Saturday on the steps of the Old Parish Church.

During the week there is a succession of band concerts, children's sports, dances, a fancy dress parade and processions. For many the highlights, of course, are the various equestrian races. The whole is rounded off with a beating retreat in the High Street on the Saturday evening.

Galashiels Gathering, end of June

Six personalities take part in this gathering, which was established in 1930. They are: the chief couple, the Braw Lad and Braw Lass; two male attendants, the Bearer of the Sod, and the Bearer of the Stone; two female attendants, the Bearer of the Red Roses and the Bearer of the White Roses.

Sunday marks the opening of the gathering with the 'Kirking of the Braw Lad', and on Monday he rides out to Lindean Kirk to place a wreath on the Preacher's Cross at a church associated with both the medieval kirk of the monks of Melrose and the Protestant Covenanters. Wednesday witnesses the main rideout to Torwoodlee, the traditional family home of the Pringles, where a sod is cut and a stone is taken from the tower. Usually there is a fancy dress parade in the evening.

On Friday comes the investiture of the Braw Lad and Lass at the Investiture Concert. Saturday's ceremonial begins with the Braw Lad receiving the burgh flag – Galashiels was created a burgh of barony in 1599 – and then he leads his riders on their first jaunt, to the Raid Stane which marks the site of a skirmish with English soldiers in 1337. Tradition has it that the English had been encamped in a grove of plum trees and that when they were vanquished at Englishman's Syke, the Galashiels folk returned in triumph waving branches of the plum trees. Indeed, a plum tree figures on the old burgh coat of arms with the motto 'soor plooms' (sour plums, also a name given to a boiled sweet long popular locally). The next visit is to Abbotsford, the home of Sir Walter Scott, to be welcomed by his descendants. The riders recross the River Tweed at Boleside and they return to Galashiels by way of Gala Hill for the ceremony at the old Town Cross. The ceremonial remembers the marriage of James IV with Margaret Tudor, the sister of Henry VIII of England, which, through James VI, ultimately led to the Union of the Crowns in 1603. The rideout is concluded at the war memorial with suitable acts of homage and loyalty to the crown. The whole is interlarded with children's sports and gymkhanas, and the last act of the gathering is the laying of a bouquet at the war memorial by the Braw Lass.

It is said that long before the Braw Lad's Gathering was contemplated the Michaelmas Fair was held at Galashiels. This was really a trade fair celebrating the town's industry and superior manhood. In his poem 'The Braw Lads O' Gala Water' (1793) Robert Burns saluted the local prowess:

> Braw, braw lads on Yarrow braes,
>   They rove amang the blooming heather;
> But Yarrow braes nor Ettrick shaws
>   Can match the lads o' Gala Water.

Reivers Week, Duns, first full week of July

This real summer festival has a riding of the bounds and four minor rideouts to watch, and follows the usual format. On the Monday evening the ceremony proper begins with the principal rider, the Reiver, being given the burgh flag for safe keeping for the week; this is followed by the first rideout round the burgh to display the flag. On Tuesday evening the Reiver leads his supporters to Duns Law, the place where the Covenanting Army of General Leslie encamped in 1639; and after a traditional address the party proceeds to the Bruntons, where the original town of Duns stood.

Wednesday afternoon sees the ceremony of the crowning of the 'Wynsome Mayde o' Dunse', which is followed by children's sports. During the evening the Reiver leads his supporters to Duns Common and on a visit to Duns Castle, the family home of the Hays. A symbolic sod is cut from the turf at Harelaw Crags and this is carried back to the town, which James IV made a burgh of barony in 1489, by way of the village of Gavinton. Thursday evening is the occasion for a rideout to Longformacus to be followed with a torchlight procession and fireworks.

On Friday the ancient game of hand ba' takes place between married men and the bachelors of the town, and the Reiver's Ball rounds off the day. The final act for the Reiver and his Lass is the Riding of the Parish Bounds, with a sports meeting on the afternoon of Saturday; and then the burgh flag is returned by the Reiver to be lodged in Duns Parish Church.

Reivers Week was established at Duns in 1949, but the Reiver is the embodiment of the medieval 'Preses of the Feuars of Duns' and down the centuries the town saw many a foray between the Scots and English. One such of 1377 is said to have given the town its motto 'Duns Dings A'' (Duns Beats Them All), and the title of the 'common riding song' which opens:

> Whae hasna read in Border lore
> That Duns o' ferlies hauds a store,
> Her Castle, Hen Poo', Bogs and Law —
> Whae disna ken that Duns dings a'?

Callants' Festival, Jedburgh, generally the first two weeks in July

Because it was so near to the Border, Jedburgh suffered regular invasions by English marauders. Although it must be said, to be quite fair, that the young men (callants) of Jedburgh's neighbourhood also made regular forays into England to pillage and steal cattle. The actual festival, though, only dates from 1947 and features the Callant as chief rider with his supporters and another personality, the Herald.

The first ride is an afternoon one on the first Saturday and this goes to Southdean, and on the following evening the Callant leads his band to Morebattle where he meets his opposite number from Kelso, the Kelso Laddie. Another ride takes place on the Thursday to Crailing, but on Saturday comes the main rideout to Redeswire, the place where the Jedburgh men did battle to aid the men of Liddesdale who had fallen foul of the English. All this took place in 1575 and it is said that at this battle the Scots bow and arrow was used for the last time. There is usually an oration given by a guest speaker on site, and the return journey is by way of Falla, where races take place, and then on to Oxnam and the last gallop home.

On Monday night the Callant and his riders re-enact the Queen's Ride, in memory of Mary Queen of Scots who rode to Hermitage Castle in 1566 to visit the wounded James Hepburn, fourth Earl of Bothwell, whom she was to marry the following year. The Tuesday night ride is to Lanton for a gymkhana, and the one on Wednesday goes to Ancrum where the festivities include a dance on the Green. The next evening the Callant takes charge of the Jedburgh flag (known as 'The Jethart Flag' in accord with local parlance) to be ready for the Festival Day which follows.

Festival Day includes rides to Ferniehirst Castle and then by Douglas Camp, Lintalee and the Capon Tree, a survivor of the great medieval Jed Forest. It is a time of gymkhanas, fancy dress and community spirit all topped off by the Jedburgh Games, which originated in 1835.

Kelso's Yetholm Ride and Civic Week, middle of July
Supported by his Right-Hand and Left-Hand men, as at Jedburgh, the Kelso Laddie leads riders on a main ride to Yetholm (Saturday) and takes part in four minor rides to various locations and a visit to nearby Floors Castle, the seat of the Duke of Roxburghe. Friday has

children's sports, showjumping and a gymkhana, and since 1961 the Whipman's Ride to the Trysting Tree, and races at Friarshaugh. For many, a great highlight are the raft races on the River Tweed at the Cobby.

Common Riding, Langholm, middle of July

An unusual feature of this common riding, which is one of the original in the history of the custom, is that the ride's principal character, the Cornet, carries the colours of the winner of the Epsom Derby. The 'Muckle Toun o' the Langholm's' common riding, which started in 1816, is preceded by two rideouts on two Saturdays before the main events; one is the Bentpath Rideout and the other is the Castle Craigs Rideout.

The main event begins at 5.00 a.m. with a journey to Whita Hill and the Hound Trail which commences at 6.30 a.m. By 8.00 a.m. the Cornet has taken the town standard into his safe keeping and a circuit of the town, which became a burgh of barony in 1621, begins with visits to the old and new towns. The customary fair is 'cried' in various parts of the parish and people assemble at Castleholm for the Cornet's Chase. The afternoon sees a whole gamut of sports, from wrestling to horse racing, and the evening is rounded off with an open-air dance. On completing the Common Riding Polka the town standard is returned by the Cornet.

Common Riding, Lauder, last Saturday in August

Another of the original common ridings, which was revived to celebrate the Coronation of George V in 1910, Lauder's celebrations begin with the usual 'Kirking of the Coronet' and proceed with a burgh flag ceremony and one rideout around Lauder Common during the week. Many side events, sports and gymkhanas take place through the week.

Coldstream Civic Week, first full week in August

Set right on the Border, Coldstream (once as famous as Gretna Green for runaway marriages), sports four rideouts during the civic week. There's a rideout to Norham, after the 'sashing' of the principal rider, the Coldstreamer, a visit to the Hirsel (the home of Lord Home of the Hirsel, the former Conservative Prime Minister) and Birgham, and another rideout to Leitholm.

But the main event is the Flodden Ride. Here, on Flodden Field, where James IV's Scottish army was vanquished in 1513, the Coldstreamer lays a wreath at the memorial and a short service of commemoration is held with an oration by a guest speaker. The usual mixture of sports and friendly gatherings are here and none is more popular than the Exiles Tea whereat all 'exiles' are invited to meet and talk.

Other places still have Riding of the Marches ceremonies. There's one at **Linlithgow** (second week in June), which dates on record from 1541 but is probably much earlier; and one at **Annan** (first Saturday in July), where it has been an annual event since 1947. Another at **Sanquhar** (third week in August) was revived in 1910 and reinstated in 1947.

5

Highland Games

Highland games are not limited to the Highlands and the 1980s saw a large and sustained increase in interest in these traditional ceremonies. Today there are around one hundred Highland games celebrated from Cowal to Ceres.

Some historians have seen the origins of the modern Highland games in an early feudal mixture of sporting entertainment and a means for clan chiefs to assess the strengths of clansmen to serve in their armies, as runners over the rough terrain, or as huntsmen.

When the proscriptions on Highland dress and culture were repealed in 1782 (the Highland Garb Act of 1746 had been a consequence of the Jacobite risings), thought was given as to how the Highland way of life could be preserved, and in 1781 the first Highland Society Gathering was held at the Falkirk Tryst (a long-established meeting of the cattle drovers). In reality the 1781 gathering was a piping competition and still today the expertise of the pipers makes them 'the true aristocrats of the games'.

There are four main parts to any Highland games. **Tossing the Caber** originates from early Highland forestry. It was noted that the easiest way to take a felled treetrunk over a burn, line of rocks, or a gulley was to up-end it and heave it so that it turned end-over-end across the obstacle. The event at the Highland games is to toss the caber (i.e. treetrunk) in this way, but in a straight line from the competitor. **Putting the Stone/Throwing the Weight/Throwing the Hammer** all seem to have derived from the expertise of the blacksmiths and farriers who wished to show their prowess at trysts alongside the soldiers. From time to time efficiency in these events leads to world champion records.

Highland dancing is very old in origin and may have derived from symbolic or mime dances of Pictish heathendom. Today there are three main set dances: the *Seann Triuthas* (the Old Trews), the *Gille Calum* (Sword Dance) and the Highland Fling, created in 1792 to honour Jean, Duchess of Gordon, and the raising of the Gordon Highlanders. Other dances for judging include reels and strathspeys.

By the reign of George IV full-scale games were being held all over Scotland with the earliest gathering, in modern times, being arranged at St Fillans, Perthshire, in 1819. It was Queen Victoria who gave the survival of the games a real boost when she attended the Braemar Gathering in 1848.

EARLY SEPTEMBER

Braemar Gathering

Because of royal patronage the Braemar Gathering is undoubtedly the leader amongst the Highland games ceremonies. It takes place at the Princess Royal and Duke of Fife Memorial Park, Braemar, and begins with a solo piping at 9.30 a.m. Herein the playing of the classical music of the *piobreachd* (pibroch) displays prize-winning natural talent and the long and arduous training needed to become accomplished. The other events begin at 10.00 a.m. The gathering had its origins in 1817 and has developed as an international occasion to include Highland dancing, tossing the caber, putting the stone, throwing the hammer, sprinting, long leap,

49

inter-services tug-o'war and relay race.

Two other Highland gatherings give the spirit of the festival and the flavour of the customs:

Argyllshire Gathering, Oban, end of August
Dating from 1872 it offers the traditional parade of local chiefs and landowners, and piping is undoubtedly the main event. Held annually during the Argyllshire Gathering, the Oban Ball is one of the highlights of the Highland social scene.

Blairgowrie Highland Games, early September
Founded in the 1880s as the Fair of Blair and concentrating on horse sales, the event was strongly patronized locally until 1938 when it lapsed, to be revived in 1974. Today the games are twinned with those of the Santa Rosa Highland Gathering in California which itself was founded in 1860. Perhaps the Blairgowrie games are the most eccentric with their 300-person tug-o'war using a 736-foot rope.

As Highland games proceedings become more and more popular with young people it is only fitting that more attention is given to the **Children's Highland Games** at Mull's Pennygate Lodge, Craignure.

LAST SATURDAY IN JUNE

Ceres Festival and Games
It must have been an emotional affair, that return from Bannockburn by the men of Ceres, Fife, who had survived the bloody contest in the marshland to the south of Stirling. To celebrate the Ceres men-at-arms, who had fought for Robert I, the Bruce, against the English, there were feasting and games that lasted for days. When news of the festivities reached the king's ears he granted the Ceres folk a charter to hold a market and games every year on the anniversary of that battle of 23–24 June 1314. Every year since then – except for the two World Wars – the Ceres festivities have been held at the village green called the Bow Butts.

Legend has it the first celebrations were organized by the local magnate Sir Robert Keith of Struthers Castle, Great Marischal of Scotland (Keith had routed the English archers with his light cavalry). And today the games are a 'mini Highland games' to remember Keith's brave men. Not far away from the scene of the main events stands a lasting stone tribute set up in 1914 in the form of a cross. It reads: 'To commemorate the vindication of Scotland's independence on the field of Bannockburn, 24th June 1314 and to perpetuate the tradition of the part taken therein by the men of Ceres'. Consequently the games are deemed the 'oldest in Scotland' and as the Bow Butts is an open area (by custom and repute it cannot be fenced off) the games are 'free'.

Mention of the Bow Butts – a name found all over Fife, from St Andrews to Kingsbarns – reminds of an event now vanished from the traditional Highland games programme, namely archery. Once, all men were expected to 'keep their eye in at the butts' in compulsory archery training. Indeed, the earliest historical reference to golf in Scotland is found during the year 1457, when James II forbade the playing of golf, and football, because it kept men away from their archery practice. St Andrews University, the oldest in Scotland, maintained the spirit of archery as a tradition and custom in Scotland during the seventeenth and eighteenth centuries by holding competitions. These were held during June each year, at the Bow Butts on the Scores, sponsored by the Faculty of Arts; the colleges of St Salvator and St Leonard also had butts in their grounds.

Dates of Highland Games
(approximate for each year)

May

14	**Gourock Highland Games** George Road, Gourock.	Playing Fields,
27	**Bathgate Highland Games** Glasgow Road, Bathgate.	Meadow Park,
	Blackford Highland Games Blackford, Perthshire.	Games Park,

51

June

3	**Strathmiglo Highland Games**
	Shotts Highland Games
4	**Airdrie Highland Games** Rawyards Park, Motherwell Street, Airdrie. Commence 1.30 p.m.
	Carrick Lowland Gathering
10	**Hawick Common Riding Games** Volunteer Park, Hawick.
	Police Gala Day & Highland Tug-o'War Championships Inverness.
11	**Forfar Highland Games** Date to be confirmed Lochside Park. 12.30 p.m.
17	**Newburgh Highland Games** Mugdrum Park, Newburgh. 1.30 p.m.
18	**Aberdeen Highland Games** Hazelhead Park. 12.30 p.m.
24	**Drumtochty Highland Games** Castle Grounds, Auchenblae, nr Laurencekirk. 1.30 p.m.
	Ceres Highland Games Oldest in Scotland.

July

1	**Caithness Highland Games** Wick. 1 p.m.
	Thornton Highland Games Thornton Public Park. 1 p.m.
2	**Dundee Highland Games** Caird Park Stadium.
	Cupar Highland Games
5	**Kenmore Highland Games** Kenmore Games Field. 6 p.m.
8	**Dingwall Highland Games** Local events commence 10.30 p.m. open events at 1 p.m.; piping at 12 noon. Jubilee Park, Dingwall.
	Inverness Highland Games Inverness.
	Forres Highland Games
	Duns Sports
9	**Arbroath Highland Games** Victoria Park. 11.30 a.m.
14	**Dunbeath Highland Games** Playing Fields, Dunbeath. 1 p.m.
15	**Invergarry Highland Games**

Inverness Highland Games
Balloch Highland Games   Local events commence 11 a.m. and open at 12 noon.
Tomintoul Highland Games   11 a.m.
St Ronans Border Games   Victoria Park, Innerleithen. Local events commence 1.30 p.m.; open events commence 2 p.m.

16   **Rosneath & Clynder Highland Games** 1 p.m.
Stonehaven Highland Games   Mineralwell Park, Stonehaven. 11 a.m.

17   **Burntisland Highland Games**   Commence 12 noon.

18   **Inveraray Highland Games**   Local events commence 10.30 a.m.; open events commence 1 p.m.

19   **Luss (Loch Lomond) Highland Gathering** Local events commence 11.30 a.m.; open events at 12.30 p.m.

20   **Mull Highland Games**   Commence 11.30 a.m.

21   **Kilchoan Highland Games**

22   **Balquhidder, Lochearnhead & Strathyre Highland Games**   Local events commence 12.30 p.m.; open events at 1.30 p.m. At Lochearnhead.
Airth Highland Games   Commence 1 p.m.
Elgin Highland Games

23   **Irvine Highland Games**
Glenrothes Highland Games   Commence 1.30 p.m.

26   **Arisaig Highland Games**

28   **Langholm Common Riding Games**   Commence 2.30 p.m.
Durness Highland Gathering   The Shore Park, Durness.

29   **Halkirk Highland Games**   Couper Park, Halkirk.
Lochaber Highland Games

30   **Aviemore International Highland Games** Granish Farm, Aviemore (off old A9). 12.30 p.m.
St Andrews Highland Games   Commence 1 p.m.

August

4	**Dornoch Highland Gathering** Local events commence 10.30 a.m.; open events at 1.30 p.m. Meadow Park, Dornoch.
5	**Inverkeithing Highland Games** Local events commence 12.15 p.m.; open events at 1 p.m.; dancing 10.30 a.m.
	Aboyne Highland Games Local events commence 10.30 a.m.; open events at 12.30 p.m.
	Caol Highland Games
	Strathpeffer Highland Games Local events commence 11.30 a.m. and open events at 1 p.m.
	Brodick Highland Games Ormidale Park, Brodick, Isle of Arran.
6	**Bridge of Allan Highland Games** Strathallan Games Park, Bridge of Allan. Commence 12 noon.
	Montrose Highland Games Montrose Links.
7	**Mallaig Highland Games**
9	**Skye Highland Games** Portree.
10	**Ballater Highland Games** Local events commence at 12.45 p.m. and open events at 1 p.m.
11	**Assynt Highland Games** Commence 12 noon.
12	**Abernethy Highland Games**
	Atholl and Breadalbane Highland Games Victoria Park, Aberfeldy. Commence 2 p.m.
13	**Galloway Games** London Road Playing Field, Stranraer.
	Perth Highland Games South Inch. Commence 12.30 p.m.
19	**Helmsdale & District Highland Games** Local events commence 11 a.m. and open events at 12 noon.
	Nairn Highland Games & People's Half Marathon.
	Bute Highland Games Bute, Isle of Rothesay.
	Crieff Highland Gathering Local events commence at 12 noon and open events at

	1 p.m.
24	**Argyllshire Highland Gathering** Oban. Commence 11 a.m.
25–26	**Cowal Gathering** Dunoon.
26	**Lonach Highland Gathering** Local events commence at 11.30 a.m. and open events at 1 p.m.
	Glenurquhart Highland Games & 16 Mile Road Race Drumnadrochit. Incorporating the Scottish Heavy Events Championships.
	Birnam Highland Games Commence 1 p.m.
27	**East Lothian Highland Games** Commence 10 a.m.

September

2	**Braemar Gathering** Commence 10 a.m.
3	**Peebles Highland Games** Whitestone Park, Peebles.
	Blairgowrie Highland Games High School Playing Fields, Blairgowrie. Commence 1 p.m.
9	**Pitlochry Highland Games** Commence 11 a.m.
10	**Falkirk Highland Games** Local events commence at 10 a.m.; open events at 1 p.m. This date to be confirmed.
16	**Invercarron Highland Games** Local events commence 10 a.m.; open events at 1 p.m.

Enquiries: Local sources of information are undoubtedly the best for these largely community events, so a call at or to any local information office would be advisable. Should there be no such facility, a query to the Scottish Tourist Board at Edinburgh might be helpful, or to the relevant area tourist board.

6

Sea Festivals

Sea-water rites and festivals are amongst the oldest customs in Scotland. For a thousand years the sea was regularly petitioned for good harvests of fish by throwing flowers, food and drink into the water to placate the gods of the sea. This had a double petitionary effect though, for the early Scots folk were also trying to deflect the bad luck omens that would bring drownings and shipwrecks. In Orkney sea-water was used to ensure a good supply of butter. A woman would be appointed by a community to act as their go-between and she would go to the shore with an empty bucket. There she watched until nine waves had dashed on the shore and at the reflux of the last she took three *gowpens* (i.e. cupped hands) of sea-water and carried them back in her bucket. The water was put into the churn with the milk to ensure a good supply of butter for that year.

All along the coast of Fife, too, the fishing villages carried out a tradition to bring good catches. In particular the fishermen of Anstruther would hand out *bakes* (ship's biscuits) to all who saw them off to the white fish waters for good luck at the fishing.

Today these are the main festivals to visit associated with the sea:

Festival of the Herring Queen, Eyemouth, late July or early August

The ancient Berwickshire fishing port of Eyemouth, situated at the mouth of the River Eye, a few miles north of Berwick-upon-Tweed, has justifiable reason to try to placate an unreliable sea.

On 14 October 1881 – ever after referred to in Eyemouth as 'Black Friday' – 189 fishermen were drowned within sight of their homes. No Eyemouth family was not personally touched by the disaster and every year at the Festival of the Herring Queen there is a thought or two for those who perished.

This festival grew out of the Fishermen's Picnic of former years. But it is rich in ceremonial symbolism of dedication to the community interest. The central figure of the ceremony is the Herring Queen, who is usually a local schoolgirl. Around mid-afternoon the ceremonial begins with the arrival of the Queen-elect by fishing boat into Eyemouth harbour, and the Queen with her 'Court' of Maids of Honour is escorted ashore by the skipper.

The Eyemouth Herring Queen is, perhaps, the modern epitome of St Ebba, the patron saint of fisherfolk of south-east Scotland. In her person, too, is the local relics of the female shaman who cast the food offerings on the water in lieu of human sacrifice, for the Herring Queen traditionally carries the emblems of fruit, corn and fish.

The Queen is crowned – usually by her predecessor – on the sward near Gunsgreen House, once the haunt of smugglers. There follows prayers and hymn singing and the Queen then tours the town.

St Monans Sea Queen Festival, mid-July

The Fife village of St Monans also holds a similar festival to the one at Eyemouth. After the Queen sails in with her two attendants and a page-boy, there is a 'crowning' and stalls and games; the whole ends the next day with a 'Kirkin' O' The Queen'.

Fishermen's Walk, Musselburgh, East Lothian, early September

Once the whole of the Lothian coastal area south of the Firth of Forth had their own festivals. Now Musselburgh is the sole survivor, sporting an end of the fishing-season festival known as the Fishermen's Walk. The festival has all the relic overtones of the Harvest-Home, but this time for the sea. Before the Welfare State's benefits, the festival was an occasion on which collections of money were taken for the poor of the fishing community. Now the festivities are run on a more self-indulgent plan.

Traditionally the streets of Musselburgh are decorated with flags and bunting, and the procession sets out from Fisherrow (Musselburgh's old fishing-quarter) and the walkers' traditional costume was that of the 'fishwife' and 'fish-callant' of about one hundred and fifty years ago. The customary end of the walk is the parkland of the former Pinkie House (now Loretto School). Musselburgh's fishing fleet has now long gone, with the herring trade, but the old symbolism of nets, lobsters, crabs, boats, creels and skulls still abound.

Fishermen's Well Festivals

Before the Reformed Church forbade them (from *circa* 1579), fisherfolk held pilgrimages to certain wells; traditions that were an extension of the more general custom of visiting certain wells (springs, pools and streams) on saints' days, quarter-days and local holidays. The intent was to seek cures for a variety of ailments and bad luck associations. Once, of course, such wells were deemed the dwellings of local deities able to work water magic, and in due course they were christianized.

Many of the pilgrimages took place in May and were associated with various rituals. What the fishermen did was to walk three times around the well, sunwise, then cast a silver coin into the water before drinking from the well. The petition for good catches, safe voyages and good luck for the fishing villages were deemed sealed when the last gulp was swallowed. Often the petitioners left a pin, a ribbon or a rag from working clothes by the well (often attached to a tree) to intensify the magic influence. The tradition was carried out in total silence, and often wells were decorated with flowers at this time.

These were the most popular 'fishermen's wells':

Our Lady of Grace Well, Orton, Speyside

St Wollak's Well, Cromarty

St Olaf's Well, Cruden Bay, Aberdeenshire. This well was thought particularly efficacious in the warding off of disease in the fishing villages and often this couplet was recited at the site:

> St Olaf's Well, low by the sea
> Where pest nor plague shall ever be.

St Fittick's Well, Bay of Nigg, south of Aberdeen. The customs associated with this well were so tenacious that even in 1630, so the Aberdeen Kirk Session *Records* tell us, local Church dignitaries had to legislate against fishermen's pilgrimages taking place, and, 'it was ordainit be the haill session in ane voce that quhatsomever inhabitants within this burgh beis find

going to Sanct Fiacke's Well in ane superstitious manner seiking health to thame selffis or bairnes, sall be
censured in penaltie and repentance in such degrie as
fornicatours ar efter tryall and conviction.'

Newhaven Sea Queen gala

'Our Lady's Port of Grace' was once the name of
Newhaven which became synonymous with the 'fish-
wives' who sold fish in East Lothian from their creels.
The characterful women in their traditional fisher garb
have long gone but the spirit of the sea lives on. This
Gala Day is geared to making funds to help local
charities. The central character is the Sea Queen, and
her entourage of Consort and Attendant, who make a
'sea trip' from Granton harbour to Newhaven pier in a
flag-bedecked boat.

Fishermen's Maunday Thursday

Maunday Thursday is the day before Good Friday in
the christian calendar and was a day of ritual for many
fisherfolk – in which they mostly watched their step in
accord with the rules of superstition. Offerings of ale and
gruel were made to the sea, largely in the west of Scotland and the Isles, in the belief that it would encourage
bumper harvests of seaweed, used on land as manure.
Thus the custom is known in Gaelic-speaking areas
as **Diardaoin a Brochain/Gruel Thursday**. Usually the
offerings were poured into the sea at midnight on the
preceding Wednesday with the incantation:

> O God of the sea
> Put weed in the drawing wave
> To enrich the ground
> To shower on us food. (*Carmina Gadelica*)

These sea-orientated festivals may also be noted:

Fraserburgh Fish Festival, late July
Aberdeen Fish Festival, late August
**Viking International Sea Angling Festival, early Septem-
ber** (Shetland)

7

More Midsummer Merrymaking

10 JUNE

White Rose Day

An important, if sad, day for all Jacobites and those romantics in whose hearts the Stuart princes live. For on this day was, and is, celebrated the birthday of Prince James Francis Edward Stuart, the only son of James VII and II and his second wife Mary of Modena. At his father's death Prince James was proclaimed King of Great Britain at the French court and all Jacobites considered him King James VIII and III. At Culloden in 1746, when James's hopes were dashed with the defeat of his son Prince Charles Edward, the white rose was sported by the Jacobite clans, and the flower entered the symbolism of the Jacobites for ever. As the ballad remembers:

> White roses under the Moon
> For the King without lands to give;
> But he reigns with the reign of June
> With his rose and his blackbird's tune,
> And he lives while Faith may live!

According to Jacobite legend the rose badge – the White Cockade – was derived from the bloom picked by Prince Charles Edward at Fassifern, Loch Eil, on the march to war after the raising of the Jacobite standard at Glenfinnan in 1745. The cockade, formed of several bows, was worn in the bonnet by men and as a corsage by Jacobite ladies.

SECOND AND THIRD WEEKS OF JUNE

St Magnus Festival, Orkney Islands

The festival has come to take on a more international role in the world of arts. It offers music, drama, fine art, film and literary events.

Bon Accord Festival, Aberdeen

Starting on a Saturday near to 17 June and running to around Sunday 25 June the festival begins with a parade. It includes band concerts, cycle races, rambles, drama, piping competitions, and a wide range of sporting activities.

Guid Nychburris Day, Dumfries

Traditionally Guid Nychburris Day – which simply means 'good neighbours day' in old Scots – is an amalgam of riding of the marches, a historical pageant, a procession of the seasons, and athletic meetings and horse races. At least that was the tone when the events were in their heyday in the 1930s. Today events vary.

The whole is intended to reflect the history of Dumfries, made a Royal Burgh *circa* 1165 by King William the Lion. The idea that on one day the folk of Dumfries would be just 'good neighbours' probably goes back to the sixteenth century in spirit, and the common riding is as old as the seventeenth century. As at other Border festive days a town song was once sung:

> Frae faur an' near
> We gaither here,
> A Loreburne's loyal blude,
> To keep wi' mirth an' graun' array
> Oor ain Dumfries Guid Nychburris Day
> Wi' richt guid nychburhude.

Rosyth Naval Days

HM Naval Base, at Rosyth, west Fife, was established following the purchase by the Admiralty in 1903 of 1248 acres of land on the north shore of the Forth. A town was developed around the dockyard to accommodate the yard's workers and their families. The naval base is open to the public each June to view British and Allied warships.

Kippen Street Fair

Revived in 1980 and based on ancient traditions, this fair is set in one of Central Scotland's most charming villages by the Forth in north Stirlingshire. It is said that the street fair started in 1663 when locals would gather to sell their wares. Today over three dozen stalls sell homemade products, crafts and bric-à-brac, while craftsmen and women give kerbside demonstrations of traditional crafts. A whole range of children's sideshows are extant, too, and displays of pipe band music.

23–24 JULY

Midsummer's Eve and Midsummer's Day

Midsummer festivals persisted long in north-eastern Scotland, and in Orkney and Shetland, as a relic of the time when the area was part of Scandinavia, or had regular contact with the Norse traders. Remembered in the far north as the Feast of Baldur, Lord of Light, Midsummer's Eve marked the approach of harvests, but also of the darkness of winter and the descent of Baldur into Asgard, the fabled city of Nordic mythology where dwelt the followers of Odin.

In many parts bonfires were lit to honour the occasion and lovers leapt hand in hand, through the flames with flowers in their hands, all to petition good luck in a future marriage. It was a water-festival too, for some rode the rivers in flower-decked boats, and the medieval Church took the day and dedicated it to John the Baptist.

The dew of Midsummer morning was deemed to have healing properties as with the 'May dew'. The late Dr Annie Dunlop found this letter, of *circa* 1630, in Register House, Edinburgh, from Annabella, Countess of Lothian, to her daughter's father-in-law, the Earl of Ancrum, in which the countess said: 'Take wheate floure and knead it with dewe gathered in the morning on Midsummer day, and make thereof a cake, the which you shall bake, and give the patient to eate of it and he shall be healed.'

Herbs, too, were considered particularly efficacious if gathered on Midsummer eve or morning, particularly *hypericum pulchrum* (St John's wort). The herb was used in the Highlands to keep away witches and their craft and was extra potent if found by accident, as the *Carmina Gadelica* reminds us:

St John's Wort, St John's Wort,
My envy whosoever, has thee.
I will pluck thee with my right hand,
I will preserve thee with my left hand.
Whoso findeth thee in the cattle-fold
Shall never be without kine.

The fishermen of the east coast transferred the bonfire rites to their own festival on 29 June, known in medieval times as St Peter's Day. This fisherman-apostle was individually petitioned by the fisher families who lit small bonfires in his honour outside their front doors.

Bannockburn Eve/Day
On Sunday 23 June 1314, the Scottish army under Robert I, the Bruce, drew up its lines at the New Park, by the Bannock Burn, to take on the might of Edward II and his English army. The battle between them spilled over into 24 June to result in a resounding Scottish victory.

It is only since the Union of the Parliaments in 1707, however, that the battle has become associated with patriotic festivals and customs. As with the massacres of Flodden (1513), Glencoe (1692) and Culloden (1746), Bannockburn has become a 'trigger word' in the Scottish psyche that stimulates 'nationalism' of various forms, both party-political and romantic. This fervour was particularly stirred up by the 1914–18 war and thereafter people have gathered at Bannockburn (usually on the Saturday nearest Midsummer day) to celebrate their national feelings.

Dundee City Festival
Starting in 1988 the Dundee City Festival is said to have 'its origins in the "grass roots" activity in Dundee which is playing such a major part in the social and economic resurgence of the Tayside capital'. It features hundreds of events, exhibitions and entertainments to appeal to all ages. Incorporated within the festival period are the Dundee Photographic Festival, the Dundee Jazz Festival, the Dundee Folk Festival, and a Festival of Football.

Stirling Festival
Within late July and early August. Concerts, sporting events, writers' festival, and guided walks to exploit

the local history, character, customs and traditions. This festival also incorporates the **Bannockburn Heritage Fayre** in late July.

Dumbarton District Festival
First started in 1985 it includes Highland games, fêtes, concerts of all kinds, tours, children's events and an international selection of folk customs.

This is the time of year too when a large number of Scottish 'galas' take place of which one is typical:

Moffat and District Gala
It usually precedes the Annual Open Show, which is a livestock and farming show, and incorporates the 'Installation of the Shepherd and the Shepherd's Lass' and the 'Crowning of the Queen of Upper Annandale'. The Shepherd and the Shepherd's Lass ceremony dates from 1950 and has been held annually ever since to emphasize the local traditions surrounding sheep farming. The Queen of Upper Annandale has been elected since 1951, and she is attended by ladies-in-waiting, train bearers and pages. It is a time of sports, fancy dress parades, torchlight processions, dances and general merrymaking.

Other gala days at which to see a variety of Scotland's customs and traditions include:

May	Kintore Gala, Aberdeenshire
	Insch Gala, Aberdeenshire
June	Lockerbie Gala, Dumfriesshire
	Buckie Gala, Banffshire
	Children's Gala, Lerwick
	Dallas Gala, Forres, Morayshire
July	Boat of Garten, Inverness-shire
	Rothiemay Gala, Banffshire
	Keith Gala, Banffshire
	Broughty Ferry Gala, Angus
	New Galloway Gala, Kirkcudbrightshire
	Thurso Gala, Caithness
August	Dornie Gala, Ross and Cromarty
	Inverurie Town Gala, Aberdeenshire

September Lamlash Gala, Isle of Arran
Dufftown Gala, Banffshire
Kingussie Gala, Inverness-shire
Nairn Gala, Nairnshire
Wick Gala, Caithness
Beauly Gala, Inverness-shire

(NB: Times and locations may vary.)

THIRD WEEK OF JULY

St Ronan's Border Games/St Ronan's Cleikum Ceremony

Down the centuries the word 'devil' has come to mean Satan, the personification of the supreme evil, the foe of the Christian God. When applied in the plural, devils are synonymous with demons, malignant entities of superhuman power, so that Satan (who has many nicknames in Scotland from 'The Earl o' Hell' to 'Auld Nick') became the Prince of Devils. Scottish folklore, custom and tradition are rich in the machinations of the devil and his minions.

Witchcraft was made illegal in Scotland in 1563. Thereafter, the belief in the devil increased in proportion to the need for political and religious scapegoats created by the 'heresy', and the folklore of the devil in Scotland increased apace with the escalating trials for witchcraft. James VI – who wrote a book on the supernatural, *Demonology* (1597) – intensified belief in the devil with his own prejudices. To the Calvinists, of course, who used belief in the devil as a political tool as had the Roman Catholics, the devil was more biblical; they took their devil from Enoch, Ephesians and Luke.

So in a land where people believed in heaven and hell as physical places, and magic, black and white, it is not surprising to find that one of the country's festivals incorporates a devil as a character. He appears in the St Ronan's Cleikum Ceremony at the small Peeblesshire town of Innerleithen. This was once a popular spa to which the sick and the hypochondriac came to benefit from the saline waters at the well of St Ronan. Undoubtedly the watering place received enormous publicity with the publication of Sir Walter Scott's novel *St Ronan's Well* in 1824.

Among the celebrated visitors to Innerleithen's spa in the mid-1820s were several members of the 'Edinburgh Six-feet Club', which consisted of forty middle- and upper-middle-class men who were all six foot tall or over. They helped found the St Ronan's Club and under their influence the St Ronan's Border Games were established. According to John Gibson Lockhart, Walter Scott's son-in-law and biographer, the management of the games was taken on by 'a club of Bowmen of the Border, arrayed in doublets of Lincoln green, with broad blue bonnets, and having the Ettrick Shepherd [the poet James Hogg] as Captain'. Initially the games took in archery, jumping, racing, wrestling, stone- and hammer-throwing.

In 1901 the Cleikum Ceremony was introduced. The object of this was to underline the traditions of the saint whose name the spa had. St Ronan was a seventh-century monk – from France or Ireland, no one is sure – who was obsessed with the devil and 'his dark majesty's interference with the life of men'. The saint was long represented (heraldically on the burgh arms) as 'cleikin' the diel by the hint leg' (catching the devil by the hind leg) with his crozier. Sir Walter Scott had this design hanging above the doorway of Meg Dod's 'Cleikum Inn' in *St Ronan's Well*.

The Cleikum Ceremony is usually preceded by the installation of Innerleithen's Standard Bearer in the tradition of the Border common ridings. The Standard Bearer is the leader of the townspeople in the enactment by the old well. At the well a schoolboy, who takes the part of St Ronan, with his retinue of 'monks', meets the official party, and the Standard Bearer drinks the spa water to monitor its continuing efficacy. The party then proceeds around the town.

By tradition the Cleikum Ceremony takes place on the following evening at an indoor meeting place. The proceedings begin with the festal song:

> Rouse ye, men of old St Ronan's,
> Gather in from hills and commons,
> Ready aye to hear the summons,
> On St Ronan's, On!

Accompanied by the 'monks' the year's St Ronan is invested with his medal of office and his pastoral staff known as the Cleikum Crozier. Traditionally St Ronan has a female assistant who is likewise invested at this time. In the presence of the Standard Bearer a tableau representing the 'cleikin' o' the deil' takes place.

In 1990 a new 'Interpretive Centre' was opened at St Ronan's Well to tell the story of the spa.

8

Lammas, Michaelmas and the Harvest Feasts

Lammas, or *Lunasdal*, was the Celtic festival of autumn, sometimes known in Scotland as 'loaf mass'. In past times the Celts celebrated it with a sacrifice to the growing energies of the soil and to Lugh, the sun god. Then, too, were the fairs of Tailltan widespread, in honour of Lugh's foster-mother; and these junkets of sports and games were mirrored all over Scotland, gradually developing as local fairs.

In some places Lammas was the time of handfasting, the season of trial marriages which lasted a year and a day. At the end of the time couples who wished to continue the marriage would appear at the next fair to proclaim the fact. Sir Walter Scott reminds us of the customs in his *The Pirate*, when he mentions the Stone of Odin, at Stenness, Orkney, through an aperture in which troths were plighted at Lammas by the clasping of hands. This developed into a time of sealing bargains and for hiring servants.

Lammas then was an occasion of promises, pledges, *saining* (healing by blessing) and fairs, and the oldest Lammas Fair to remain is held at St Andrews.

EARLY AUGUST

Lammas Fair, St Andrews

From medieval times St Andrews had markets on Mondays and Thursdays, but the five great annual fairs held more importance. These were Candlemas, the Easter Senzie Fair, Lammas itself, Martinmas, and St Andrew's Day.

The only surviving fair of medieval origin is the Lammas Fair, also known as Lammas Market. Today it is a brash and noisy anachronism that obstructs Market Street and South Street. The fair/market was secured as a privilege in 1620 by James VI and I and it was confirmed as a burgh right by the Act of Parliament of Charles I. It was the Victorian and Edwardian hiring fair for the district. Today street barkers have taken over from the old provisions stalls, and the cacophony of generators have superseded the steam engines and horsepower which once drove the fairground features.

Inverkeithing's Hat and Ribbon Race

Inverkeithing's Lammas Fair was revived in 1964. It is mentioned in 1652 as being a day of 'fun, frolic, fit races, ale and drunken fools', and it drew people from a large area around. Certainly the fair was established in some form by the fifteenth century, as James IV bought some of his horses here.

An integral part of the fair is the Hat and Ribbon Race which itself seems to date from the seventeenth century. It is run on the Friday evening of the fair. The race itself is preceded by a procession led by a pipe band, a district officer, who holds aloft a top hat decorated with ribbons, and a group of local and district representatives. The event began as a race for herdsmen, with a prize of a hat, with ribbons for the winning herdsman's 'lass'.

Pittenweem Festival

This festival was started in 1981 and has become an important part of the community year. It incorporates a mix of events which include celebrating yesterday's fishing trade, a craft fair, opera and exhibitions.

One recurrent theme is the Fife village's marine history and one event gives a flavour of the overall motif, as described in a recent programme:

> The Press Gang will be sailing into Pittenweem harbour tonight to enlist the local fishermen into His Majesty's Navy. The year is 1789 and rumours of John Paul Jones in the Firth of Forth have reached Pittenweem. Townspeople and allies are requested to gather at the top of the Braes to lead a torchlit procession along the High Street and down to the harbour to meet the Press Gang. Will Pittenweem lose its finest menfolk to the Press Gang or will John Paul Jones create the necessary diversion to save the day? – Join and find out.

A very popular local location for events is St Fillan's Cave, traditionally recognized as the chapel and dwelling of the seventh-century saint of that name.

Victoria Week, Ballater, Royal Deeside

Not long after her accession to the throne of Great Britain, Queen Victoria bought Balmoral. Her regular visits to the area developed 'Royal Deeside', and Ballater became the railway terminus at which she and members of her family alighted for their journeys to and from Balmoral Castle. This festival celebrates Ballater's long association with Queen Victoria and incorporates craft fairs, music recitals, children's entertainment, dance displays, fancy dress, funfairs, and a replay of Victorian customs.

The Burryman, South Queensferry

South Queensferry's strange custom has all the camouflage of a fertility rite. Yet folklorists believe that that line of research is a red-herring. Sir Walter Scott spent some time investigating the origins of the Burryman, but drew a blank. Today the origins are still shrouded in mystery. Whatever the derivation of the Burryman, he has been making his walk for hundreds of years. Queensferry, a royal burgh (1364) from the days of David II, has had a ferry fair of one kind or another since the 1400s.

The Burryman has a gruelling day, and must be fit. A candidate for the office qualifies if he is a native of South

Queensferry. It takes three hours to dress the man in his famous costume of burrs (*Arctimus Bandana*) and the Burryman is on the go from nine in the morning to six in the evening. He is clad in woollen jersey from head to foot, and on this material the burrs are stuck. His hat is decked with fresh roses, of which there are more blooms on shoulders and waist, just above the Union Jack which girdles the Burryman. Two attendants carrying torch-like garlands accompany the Burryman as he is virtually blind behind his face mask of burrs. Both preceded and followed by cheering children, the Burryman walks around South Queensferry, collecting drams while the children rattle collecting tins to cover expenses. As he walks the streets, the Burryman stops to talk to passers-by and is invited indoors, to both commercial and private houses; some old folk averred that it is unlucky if the Burryman does not make a personal visit.

The Ferry Fair opens up beside the Hawes Inn – immortalized by Robert Louis Stevenson in *Kidnapped* – and here the Burryman pauses to take a long rest. In all it is said that he walks nine miles in his cumbersome and heavy suit (his hat traditionally weighs around seven pounds). The Ferry Fair has a variety of customs and events, from pram races to clambering up a greasy pole. The Ferry Queen presents the prizes in the various competitions.

It is possible that the Burryman image is based upon a folk-memory of the once-petitioned spirits of vegetation in nature worship, with a vague memory of the traditional village scapegoat (who is believed to carry away all the year's evil from a community). Some aver that the Burryman is a relic of a ritual character who was petitioned when there was a poor fishing season.

Festival of 'Horse and Boys' Ploughing Match, St Margaret's Hope, Orkney

The pioneer Viking settlers sailed their longships across uncharted seas around Britain's northern coastline in the eighth and ninth centuries. Their reputation stains them now as bloodthirsty marauders, but in reality they were farming folk in search of new land. Ever since, the customs and traditions of the Orkneys and Shetlands have been touched with the Norsemen's dowry of belief.

Since Viking days the lives of the Orcadian farmers have been unpredictable, and magic ritual was one of the arcane arts a farmer had to practise if his crops and cattle were to be saved from the evil spirits which flew in on the east wind (i.e. the way the Vikings had come). No Orcadian cattleman would have an odd number of cows, that was bad luck; he would rather buy or sell some stock to keep the number even. When a cow had a calf a fire was kindled near the byre to keep away the trows, the supernatural creatures who lived underground, or in the hollow hills – the Vikings called them the *underjordiske*. And the whole range of Nordic customs, traditions and festivals were defensive in tone against the supernatural. Again, before the first furrow was cut in spring, the ploughmen smeared urine over the ploughs and tied a thin round stone to the plough beams; obviously symbols of the sun and fertility. Still today at St Margaret's Hope, South Ronaldsay, takes place a very old custom, the Ploughing Match during August. In this tradition the 'horses' are barbarically dressed youngsters and the 'ploughmen' are their chosen mates.

In her piece on the subject, Rhoda Spence describes the traditional 'horses':

> The horses on display each year are brightly decked with colour and sparkle. Faces of dumpling innocence are framed between curiously exotic-looking head-dresses and horsecollars which are thickly trimmed with anything that will catch the light – pearl buttons, spangles, mirror glass, gold braid, tiny bells. To these are added ribbons and feathers. Sleeves are closely decorated, and the sturdy legs, which bear such testimony to the goodness of the country food, sport knee frills, cross garters, and, of course, hair anklets to resemble a horse's fetlocks. Sometimes the horses wear tails, and the edges of their shoes are painted to simulate horseshoes.

After gathering at a public place where the horse costumes are judged, the party leaves for the beach at Sand o' Right where sections have been set out for ritual ploughing. With replica ploughs the 'ploughmen' make furrows in the sand. Games and dancing usually follow the ploughing.

Other August festivals of note

Faultline Festival, various venues, Inverness
Grantown-on-Spey Summer Festival
Dundee Water Festival
Skye Folk Festival, Portree, Isle of Skye
Lourin Fair, Old Rayne, Aberdeenshire
Aberdeen Fish Festival

SEPTEMBER

Arbroath Abbey Pageant, early September

This colourful pageant does not occur very often, but when it does it is one of Scotland's most spectacular customs. The abbey of Arbroath, once administered by Benedictine monks of the Tironesian Order from France, founded by King William the Lion in 1178 and dedicated to Thomas the Martyr of Canterbury, stands in the heart of the Angus burgh. These days it is a popular tourist haunt, but the stately ruin is the magnificent backcloth for the pageant which stirs the heart of every patriotic Scot. For here took place in 1320 an event which was one of the most momentous in Scottish history, the signing of the Declaration of Independence which was a consequence of the defeat of Edward II's army at Bannockburn in 1314. The Declaration was inspired and composed by Bernard de Linton (died 1331), Abbot of Arbroath and Chancellor of Scotland. Abbot Bernard was a friend and counsellor of Robert I, the Bruce, King of Scots (1274–1329), who used his great talents to put forward Robert I's case for recognition.

For Robert I to be recognized as a king among kings in Europe it was necessary for him to be acknowledged as such by the Pope. Alas for Scotland, Pope John XXII had aligned himself with England. In 1320 he threatened to excommunicate the whole of the Scottish nation from Christendom unless they recognized Edward II as their Lord Paramount. The Scots refused and Bruce himself defied the Pope, who had summoned him to appear before him at Avignon. Instead the Scots held a parliament at Arbroath and drew up their famous Declaration on 6 April. The Declaration, described as one of the noblest ever to be drawn up by human hand, took the form of a letter to the Pope. Its wording was courteous and reverent, yet it made the points clearly that the Scottish nation would not stand for interference in its liberties even from 'the Most Holy Father in Christ'.

The Scots peace and freedom, the Declaration averred, had been disturbed by Edward I who had 'harried most spitefully our realm without a ruler'. Following the Battle of Dunbar, 27 April 1296, Scotland had become a vassal lordship with many Scots nobles held ransom in England. The country had been liberated by Robert I and they now looked to the Pope to cast 'a tender and fatherly eye upon the calamities and straits brought upon us and the Church of God by the English'. As their words resounded in Latin around those assembled in the great hall of the Palais des Papes in Avignon, commentators said that the Pope was noticeably moved. 'It is not for glory, riches or honour that we fight,' Abbot Bernard had written, 'it is for liberty alone, the liberty which no good man loses but with his life.'

After due deliberation the Pope wrote to Edward II and urged reconciliation and peace with the Scots. By the Treaty of Northampton (1328), Edward II declared that 'the Kingdom of Scotland shall remain firm forever to the great prince, Lord Robert, by the Grace of God, illustrious King of Scotland, and to his heirs and successors.'

The commemoration of this great event in pageant form was initiated in Arbroath in 1947 with a re-enactment of the momentous signing as the highlight. The pageant fell into abeyance in 1955 but was reinstated in 1964, and was performed in 1980. Today the pageant would include the characters of Abbot Bernard, King Robert, the Bishops of Dunkeld, Aberdeen and St Andrews, mounted barons, singing monks, acolytes and soldiers. Following a prayer of dedication *The Prologue*, written by J. Crawford Milne, is spoken by a man-at-arms. It begins:

On this quiet spot let us take breath
And rest awhile from present cares
That strong oppress the world.
So may we scan this country that we love,
This Scotland into which we were most haply
    born,
And bring it to that spirit deep within
From which our race has drawn its strength . . .

There follows the play, written by F.W.A. Thornton, called *The Laurel Crown*, depicting the trial of Sir William Wallace (1272–1305), the outlawed Scottish knight who became the champion of Scottish independence in defiance of Edward I. The scene is Westminster Hall, London, 1305. Then comes the signing of the Declaration. It is a pageant of colour, light, music and rhetoric to celebrate a noble declaration of Scottish spirit. The pageant can only take place these days when the Pageant Society raises the necessary funds.

Largs Viking Festival, mid-September
The festival was begun in 1980 and commemorates the Battle of Largs which took place in the autumn of 1263. On that occasion a massive Viking fleet, led by the celebrated Norwegian King Haakon Hakonson the Old, appeared in the neighbourhood on an aggressive expedition to prop up his possessions in the Hebrides. He was repulsed by an army of Scots on the slopes of the Cunningham Hills; the place was celebrated evermore and Largs takes its name from the word meaning 'the slopes'. In truth, a freak storm routed the Norse armada, but it was to mark a turning point in Scotland's destiny. One direct result was that the Western Isles, long a part of Norse territory, became a region of the Scottish realm.

One of the main objectives of the festival is to remember and pay tribute to the age of the Vikings through exhibitions, lectures and re-enactments of the battle. Its international aim is to make lasting cultural links with Scandinavia.

Michaelmas
The Feast of Michaelmas, 29 September, celebrates the dedication of St Michael the Archangel, leader of

the Heavenly Host. He was the patron of fishermen and horsemen, and in the west of Scotland and the Hebrides, Michaelmas was the great festival time of the year. It was a time to celebrate with horse-races and the giving of gifts, including carrots, which were harvested and blessed at this time. The inferences of a 'harvest festival' were also upheld with the baking of a *Struan Micheil* (St Michael's Struan), a special cake made from the year's cereals. Harvest Home, by the by, as a festival in Scotland was most celebrated in Gaelic-speaking Scotland and the north-east.

Other events of September to note
Dundee Autumn Festival
Peebles Art Festival
Melrose Folk Festival
Autumn Festival, Dufftown

9

The Rites and Customs
of Hallowe'en

The Eve of All Hallows, 31 October, known as Hallowe'en, was entered on the Christian calendar as the Feast of All Saints, the 'Commemoration of all the Faithful Departed'. In accordance with the practice of the early Christians in Scotland, this festival was transplanted on to a pagan one, the Celtic festival of Samhuinn, in fact. But for a thousand years before Albert Einstein anticipated the fourth dimension, the Celts had invested in this night the occasion when the past, the present and the future become one. They celebrated with bonfires at dusk.

Samhuinn was the winter solstice (the point in the ecliptic at which the sun is furthest south of the equator) when the Celts returned their flocks to the protection of the winter fold. Thus Samhuinn was a day of thanksgiving to the gods for the safe return of the cattle, and a petitioning for the renewal of the food supply for the year. Certain of the Celtic customs of this time of year survive as modern Hallowe'en symbols or rites.

The Celts Samhuinn was also a feast of the dead, in the season of earth's decay, so it was easy to graft it on to All Saints. Hallowe'en came to be regarded as a time when evil walked, as well as good. Sir Walter Scott remembered this as a time to be vigilant:

On Hallowmas Eve, ere ye boune to rest,
Ever beware that your couch be blest;
Sign it with cross and sain it with bead,
Sing the Ave and the Creed.

For on Hallowmas Eve the Nighthag shall ride,
And all her nine-fold sweeping on by her side,
Whether the wind sing lowly or loud,
Stealing through moonshine or swathed in a
      cloud.

> He that dare sit in St Swithin's Chair
> When the Nighthag wings the troubled air,
> Questions three, when he speaks the spell,
> He must ask and she must tell.

Needless to say Hallowe'en was the night of witches' great conventicles, or 'sabbats'. Old folk said that after dark on this day witches could be seen flying through the air on broomsticks and eggshells, or thundering over field and mountain on black cats and black horses, in the mad Hallowmas Ride. In some places bonfires were lit on this night to deflect the witches' ride and on them was burned the figure of a witch as a 'guy'.

It was also deemed the time when fairy folk made a mass migration from fairy hillock to fairy hillock. With them they took those mortals they had kidnapped. So Hallowe'en was a time when the unfortunates could be snatched back by their loved ones. Thus in 'The Young Tamlane', in his *The Minstrelsy of the Scottish Border*, Sir Walter Scott has Janet win back her love:

> This nicht is Hallowe'en Janet,
> The morn is Hallowday;
> And, gin ye daur your true luve win,
> Ye hae nae time to stay.
>
> The nicht it is gude Hallowe'en,
> When faerie folk will ride;
> And they that wad their true luve win,
> At Miles Cross they maun bide . . .
>
> Gloomy, gloomy was the nicht,
> And eerie was the way,
> As fair Janet, in her mantle green
> To Miles Cross she did gae . . .
>
> About the dead hour o' the nicht
> She heard the bridles ring;
> And Janet was as glad o' that,
> As ony earthlie thing . . .
>
> And first gaed by the black, black steed
> And then gaed by the broun,
> But fast she gript the milk-white steed
> And pu'd the rider doun . . .

She shaped him in her arms at last,
A mother-naked man;
She wrapt him in her green mantle,
And sae her true luve won.

To the superstitious all the clues were there; the green mantle and the 'mother-naked man' symbolizing rebirth, and the 'milk-white steed' the good omen to be sought against the bad ('the black, black steed').

From the orgiastic rites of *Samhuinn* have developed the antics of modern Hallowe'en. Bonfires and the ritual burning of witches were once tenacious customs. The chief characters of Hallowe'en are the guisers, who used to perform a play called *The Goloshan* (cf pagan *ludus*). Today they remain the direct descendants of the masked men of Druidic times who disguised themselves (i.e. in guises) so as not to be recognized by the spirits of the dead, and thus be trapped in the limbo between this world and the next. Instead of masks some guisers blackened their faces – a Druidic relic of smearing the body with ashes, for occult protection. These days the practices of the guisers have passed almost entirely to children.

The main symbol of Hallowe'en is the turnip lantern. The scooped-out turnip is traditionally given a skull-like face, with a candle set inside to enhance the ghostly effects. The whole was meant to ape the skulls set up around a tribal fire to keep evil demons away.

Divination was an important part of this festival of omens and auguries. Those who had the power 'to see things' denied to ordinary mortals were much petitioned at this time for prognostications.

One of the outstanding pieces of Scottish literature to describe the custom of Hallowe'en is the poem of that name written by Robert Burns in 1786. In it he describes the customs of kale pulling, selecting stalks of corn, the Sweetheart Nuts, clew throwing, apple at the glass, sowing hempseed, the wecht ceremony, the Stack to faddom't thrice and the Three Luggies.

For the first Hallowe'en act of divination, the diviner, with closed eyes, went into a field of kale (cabbage) and pulled a plant at random; the size, length and shape could all be 'read' to ascertain a future spouse's identity. Its taste indicated a sweet nature or an acid temper, and the stalk was placed above a doorway to divine the christian name of the intended (the first person to pass under the stalk would be that person or have the same name). Stalks of corn were pulled too, to divine the morality of a future spouse (grains missing meant an immodest character). A *clew* was a piece of yard thrown into the kiln pot; this would slowly form, it was thought, into the initial letter of the future lover's name. Sow hempseed, repeat the words: 'Hemp seed I saw thee, Hemp seed I saw thee', look over your left shoulder and you would see your love 'in the attitude of pulling hemp'.

Burns himself explained the wecht ceremony thus:

This charm must likewise be performed, unperceived and alone. You go to the barn, and open both doors; taking them off the hinges, if possible; for there is a danger, that the Being, about to appear, may shut the doors, and do you some mischief. Then take that instrument used in winnowing the corn, which, in our country-dialect we call a wecht; and go through all the attitudes of letting down corn against the wind. Repeat three times; and the third time, an apparition will pass through the barn, in at the windy door, and out at the other, having both the figure in question and the appearance or retinue marking the employment or station in life.

And of the 'Stack to faddom't thrice' he said this: 'Take an opportunity of going, unnoticed, to a bear-stock, and fathom it three times round. The last fathom of the last time, you will catch in your arms, the appearance of your future conjugal yoke-fellow.'

As the divining of the future state of matrimony was uppermost in the minds of the young, The Three Luggies custom was a must, noted Burns. Here's what had to be done. Three luggies (small dishes with 'lugs', or handles) were placed in a row on a table or hearth. Into one was placed clear water, into another sooty water and the third was left empty. The diviner, blindfold, was led to the luggies, where an attempt was made to dip the left hand into one of the dishes. If the performer (usually male) chanced upon the dish of clear water, he was deemed to marry a virgin; if he chanced on the foul water, then he would marry a widow or an unchaste woman would be his lot; if the empty dish was chosen, he would remain a bachelor. The ritual could only take place three times (a session) before the oracle lost its potency.

The Sweetheart Nuts were another form of love/marriage divination. Two groups of hazel-nuts were placed before a fire. One group would be given the name of bachelors and the other the names of spinsters within a parish. As the nuts 'popped' the names were romantically linked.

The apple might well be deemed to be the fruit of Hallowe'en in Scotland, being used for both divination and for the 'dookin'', ritual. A large wooden tub half-filled with water would be placed in the middle of the floor. Into this would be tossed some well-polished apples. In turn the company would kneel at the tub and try to seize an apple in the teeth without using hands. Alternatively the operator would hold a fork between the teeth and attempt to spear an apple by dropping the fork into one. This is a relic of the Druidic Ordeal by Water, signifying the passage of the soul across the waters to the hereafter, to Apple-land (Avalon). Burns's 'apple at the glass' custom he remembered thus: 'Take a candle, and go, alone, to a looking glass: eat an apple before it, and some traditions say you should comb your hair all the time: the face of your conjugal companion to be, will be seen in the glass, as if peeping over your shoulder.'

10

St Andrew, Scottish Saints and their Festivals

St Andrew, as a symbol of Scotland's individuality and nationhood, was engraved on the great seal of Scotland's government after the death of Alexander III in 1286, and on the gold 'lion' coins of Robert III (1390–1406). Thereafter the apostle and martyr was closely associated with the spirit of Scotland, although the symbol of his martyrdom as a national badge belongs to the tenth century in Scotland.

The figure of St Andrew and his story were well known in Scotland from the eighth century, both from legend and from the gospel of St John, which tells how Andrew of Bethsaida in Galilee walked with Our Lord and introduced his brother Simon Peter to Him. Andrew was the first Christian missionary who carried Christ's gospel to Byzantium, that ancient Greek city, which under its later name of Constantinople became the capital of the eastern Roman Empire. For his work Andrew suffered a lingering martyrdom at Patras, in Achaia, bound, it is said, by the order of the Roman proconsul Aegates, on the distinctive cross which was to be associated with him, the *crux decussata* (X-shaped). This was *circa* 30 November in the year AD 60.

The apostle's cadaver lay at Patras for about 300 years, when the Christian convert Emperor Constantine decided to make his capital at old Byzantium. Here too he wished to establish a centre of Christianity and ordered that Andrew's body be transferred to his new city, Constantinople. At this point, so the legend has it, a portion of Andrew's bones were transferred to Scotland.

There are two versions of the story of how Andrew's bones came to Scotland. Version one dates from around 1165 and tells us how Pictish High King Angus (731–61) was raiding in the Merse (today's Berwickshire, Borders Region) when he came across a hostile army from the south. While walking with his earls, Angus saw a flashing and blinding light and heard the voice of the Apostle Andrew telling him to challenge the hostile army, for if he held aloft the cross of Christ he would surely have victory. This he did and won the battle. At the same time, the legend recounts, an angel was guiding corporeal relics of St Andrew from Constantinople to a landing place which is now known as St Andrews. The guardian of these relics was one Rule or Regulus, a Greek monk. Angus met Rule and promised that he would honour St Andrew and have a shrine set up to him at his fortified encampment at Cennrigmonaid, which we now call St Andrews.

The second version of the story dates from around 1279 and also tells of St Rule, or St Regulus, having been warned that Constantine was to remove the body of the apostle to Constantinople, bringing corporeal relics of St Andrew out of Patras. These relics are listed as a tooth, a kneecap, an upper arm-bone and three fingers from the apostle's right hand. These relics were said to have been brought by Rule to 'the utmost part of the world' a place called Muckross, 'the headland of the boars', soon to be called Kilrymont, an early name for St Andrews. Both versions have evidence of monkish hands, written to show the importance of the religious site at St Andrews then being evolved as the location of a new cathedral and priory *circa* 1143–60. After the fall of Constantinople, by the by, in 1204 St Andrew's bones were taken by crusaders to Amalfi and his head to Rome; it was returned to Constantinople by Pope Paul VI.

In Scotland the Feast of St Andrew — Anermas — was as important as that of St Peter, and today the festival is celebrated all over the world with dinners and expatriate junketings with the toast, 'To the memory of St Andrew and Scotland Yet'. Special dinners to celebrate the saint, outwith religious ceremonies that is, were old when Sir David Lyndsay (1486–1555), Lyon King of Arms, wrote in the *Historie of Squyer Meldrum* of how James IV held such a dinner:

> And ilk year for his Patron's saik,
> Ane banquet royall walk he maik,
> With wylde fowle, venisoune and wyne,
> With tairt and flam and fruitage fyne;
> Of bran and geill there was na skant,
> And ypocras he wald not want.

The verse may be translated into modern parlance as: Every year for the sake of his patron (saint), he would organize a royal banquet. There was no lack of wild foul, venison, wine, tarts and custards and fine fruit, brawn and jelly (from roast beef). Neither did the king want for Hippocras (a type of spiced wine).

It is fitting that the saint is remembered annually on 30 November with a full day's celebrations in the town that bears his name. The St Andrew's Day programme at St Andrews usually begins with a community breakfast, a religious service at Holy Trinity Church, a lecture, and various musical and dramatic events at different locations in the burgh. The whole is overseen by the St Andrew's Society of St Andrews, founded in 1980.

CALENDAR OF SAINTS' FEASTS AND CUSTOMS IN SCOTLAND

This is a selective listing of Scotland's main customs and festivals associated with Scottish saints both by birth and adoption. The counties, towns and villages mentioned all held local feasts and fairs in honour of their saintly patrons.

January

8 (and 19):   St Nathalan, bishop, died 678. Many parts of Aberdeenshire.

9 (and 19):   St Fillan, abbot, died 734. Loch Earn and elsewhere.

13:   St Kentigern, also named Mungo, bishop, died 603. Glasgow.

20:   St Fechan, died 664. Celebrated at St Vigeans, Arbroath and Ecclefechan, Dumfries. **St Agnes's Eve**: Held mostly in the north of Scotland when young folk of both sexes undertook divination customs. At midnight they would go to a cornfield and throwing handfuls of grain in the air would recite:

> Agnes sweet and Agnes fair,
> Hither, hither now repair,
> Bonnie Agnes, let me see,
> The lad (or lass) who is to marry me.

Once they had returned home, the psychic 'shadow' of that person they were to marry (supposedly) appeared in a mirror.

February

1:   St Bride of Kildare, abbess, died *circa* 525. Feast held in Gaelic Scotland on the old Celtic festival of spring. Thus there was a fusion of pagan and Christian rites. The Bonnetmakers' Craft (one of the nine incorporated trades) of Dundee elected their Deacon on St Bride's Day.

6:   St Baldren, died 608. East Lothian.

18:   St Colman, Bishop of Lindisfarne, died 676. South Scotland.

23:   St Boisil, Prior and Abbot of Melrose, died 664. Border counties.

March

1:   St Ernan, also named Ennoc, died 625. Kilmarnock. St Monan, seventh-century missionary. Centre of a harvest thanksgiving at St Monans, Fife.

8:   St Duthac, Bishop of Ross, died 1065. East coast of Scotland, particularly Tain.

10: St Kessoc, bishop (patron of Scotland before St Andrew), died in battle in 560. Lennox and south Perthshire.

17: St Patrick, bishop, Apostle of Ireland, said to have been born at Dumbarton in 373. One of the 'Seven Champions of Christendom' who appeared in Scottish guiser traditions, died 463.

20: St Cuthbert, Bishop of Lindisfarne, died 687. South Scotland.

22 (and 10 Sept): St Finian of Morville, died 578. South-west Scotland, particularly Kilwinning and Kirkgunzeon.

30: St Regulus, possibly Rieul, Bishop of Senlis. Third century. (See St Andrew.)

April

1: St Gilbert, Bishop of Caithness, died 1245. Dornoch.

16: St Magnus Erlendsson, killed 1117. Egilsay, Orkney, Kirkwall.

17: St Donan, killed 616. Feasted in north and west Scotland, and particularly at Kildonan, Sutherland.

May

12: St Comgall of Bangor and Tiree, died 603.

16: St Brendan the Voyager, patron saint of Bute, *circa* 484–577.

June

10: St Margaret of Scotland, wife of Malcolm Canmore, *circa* 1045–93. Celebrated all over Scotland, with services at her shrine in Dunfermline Abbey and at her chapel in the south transept of St Andrews Cathedral. Her main feast was held in Scotland on 16 November.

12: St Ternan, early bishop of the Picts, *circa* fifth century. Central Scotland.

25: St Molic (or Moluag), pupil of St Brendan, sixth century. Missionary to Argyll and the Isles.

July

1: St Serf, probably a slave brought from the Gaelic west, tutor of St Kentigern. The centre of his cult was at Culross, Fife, in which abbey he was buried. Up to the 1860s a procession in honour of St Serf was extant in Culross, wherein local burgesses marched bearing eleven green branches on his feast day.

11:   St Drostan, Abbot of Deer, Aberdeenshire *circa* 610.

15:   St Donald, of Ogilvy, Forfar. On the death of his wife, Donald's nine daughters formed a religious community. They were celebrated on 18 July at the **Feast of the Nine Maidens**, a popular junket in Angus.

18:   St Thenew, daughter of Loth, King of Lothian, and mother of St Kentigern, sixth century. Celebrated in Fife and Lothian.

29:   St Olaf, King of Norway, *circa* 995–1030. Feasted in the far north. **St Peter's Fair, Biggar**. This festival was held mid-July, near to the 29th in honour of Simon Peter, brother of St Andrew, who was a fisherman of Bethsaida. The fair dated from the sixteenth century wherein were incorporated a 'Ba' Game and Foot Race'; in the latter a pair of gloves were given (up to 1843) to the winner. The event was later incorporated into the day of the horse parade held by the Whipmen. A Gala Day remains as a relic of the original festival.

August

5:   **St James's Fair, Kelso**. On the triangle of land between Tweed and Teviot, to the west of modern Kelso, stood the now vanished capital of Scotland, the burgh of Roxburgh, whose ancient ruined castle still dominates the western aspect. Here, on Friar's

Haugh, was held St James's Fair, named after St James the Less, the dedicatees of the nearby abbey of the Benedictine monks from Tiron, France. This fair was once a magnet for gypsies who, during the fair, had camping and grazing rights on Friar's Haugh. Because of their presence the fair developed into a horse market.

11: St Blane, bishop, *circa* 590. Celebrated in Bute, Lennox and Dunblane.

18: St Inan, evangelist, ninth century. Feasted in Ayrshire where a local holiday was called after him as St Inan's or Tenants' Day.

20: St Ronald, Earl of Orkney, killed 1158. Celebrated in the northlands.

Mid-August: St Barchan's Day, also known as Lilias Day. St Barchan was a sixth-century Irish missionary famed for his cell at Kilbarchan, Renfrewshire. The name Lilias comes from the name of Lilias Cuninghame, of the family of the Earl of Glencairn, who became the central 'queen' of the ceremony. A third character in the festivities was Habbie Simpson, a famous local piper and humorist. The poet Robert Semple of Beltrees wrote this of Habbie:

> Sae kindly to his nychburris neist
> At Beltane and St Barchan's feast
> He blew, and then held up his briest
> As he war weid . . .

This festival may have been of late eighteenth-century origin, but it died out in the 1890s, to be resuscitated in 1931, to go into desuetude again in 1955.

25: St Ebba the Elder, abbess of Coldingham, died 683. Favoured in the south-east Borders.

27: St Maol Rubha, *circa* 640–722. Celebrated in the north and west of Scotland, in particular at Loch Maree, Ross-shire. **Summereve's Fair**, Keith, Banffshire, was dedicated to him.

30: St Fiacre, sixth century. A Columban monk, celebrated in the north and west of Scotland, but who went as a missionary to France. He was a particular favourite in the parish of St Fittick's, Nigg, Aberdeen and is remembered as the patron saint of gardeners.

September

1: St Giles. A shadowy saint who is said to have come from Greece to evangelize France some time in the sixth to eighth centuries. Giles was the patron saint of cripples, beggars and blacksmiths, as well as that of Elgin and Edinburgh.

15: St Mirren, Abbot of Bangor, and regionary bishop, seventh century. The patron saint of Paisley.

16: St Ninian lived during the fourth and fifth centuries and was the disciple of another saint popular in Scotland, St Martin of Tours. Ninian was the founder of the religious community known as Candida Casa, which later developed as Whithorn Abbey. His fame as an evangelist made him celebrated in south-west Scotland, particularly around his shrine and along the Galloway coast.

23: St Adamnan of Donegal, *circa* 624–704. He is famous as a scholar – he wrote *The Life of St Columba* – and was buried at Iona.

25: St Barr, Bishop of Cork, a sixth-century Irish evangelist. Barra takes its name from this saint.

October

7: St Syth, the little-known cleric who was celebrated at Kilsyth, south Stirlingshire, and remembered as the patron saint of lost or mislaid goods.

8: St Triduana, buried at Restalrig, Edinburgh.

13: St Comgan, eighth-century figure who founded a community at Lochalsh, and was feasted in Argyll and Turriff in particular; buried at Iona.

18: **The Feast of St Luke**, named after the first-century evangelist, who according to tradition was a Syrian from Antioch and a physician. He is called 'the beloved physician' in the Epistle to the Colossians. St Luke's memory is still feasted at a dinner and orations by the Scottish Arts Club of Edinburgh. The Feast of St Luke was also called Sour Cakes Day, particularly in the west of Scotland. *The New Statistical Account of Rutherglen* (1836), has this comment: 'The most famous fair of Rutherglen was St Luke's in October, and was signalled by making cakes. About eight or ten days before the fair, a quantity of oatmeal is made into a dough with warm water and laid up in a vessel to ferment.'

25: St Crispin, died 287. As the patron saint of shoe-makers he was celebrated by the medieval shoemakers' guilds in various Scottish burghs. Processions, local events and pageants were held in his name. During New Year the shoemakers of Aberdeen had a special 'walk' to honour him.

November

6: St Leonard, the Frankish founder of the monastery of Noblac, France, died 560. Patron saint of St Andrews (with St Andrew), and of women in childbirth, prisoners and locksmiths. The College of St Leonard and St Andrews was founded in 1512 on the relics of an early medieval hospice for pilgrims.

11: St Martin, Bishop of Tours, *circa* 315–97, a Hungarian pagan converted to Christianity. **The Feast of Martinmas**, named after this patron of rustics, was a Scottish quarter-day when farm labourers (and others) were paid their quarterly fees, and when some sought new employment. **The Eve of St Martin** was the time when household parties were held to mark the quarter-day. The feast was undoubtedly grafted on to festivities associated with *Samhuinn* in which salted meat was laid down for winter consumption, and was celebrated all over Scotland.

12: St Machar, sixth-century Irish missionary, first Bishop of the Scots and patron saint of Aberdeen.

13: St Devenick, a fifth-century evangelist little known in the hagiology of Christianity, buried at Banchory-Devenick. Honoured in Caithness and Sutherland.

18 (sometimes 27): St Fergus, sixth- (or eighth-) century evangelist, probably Bishop of the Scots; founded Glamis church. Celebrated in Scotland's east coast and northern counties from Angus to Caithness.

22: St Cecilia, patrician Roman, patron saint of music.

December

6: St Nicholas of Bari, Bishop of Myra in the fourth century. Pageants and mummery in his honour.

St Nicholas Festival, Winter Gardens, Duthie Park, Aberdeen still takes place.

14: St Drostan, disciple of St Columba of Deer, *circa* 610.

10: **St Obert's Play**, Perth. This now defunct festival was centred on the patron saint of bakers, on whose Eve the bakers would parade around the streets of Perth in disguises. The central figure was a mounted St Obert; the pageant was forbidden after the Reformation as 'popish'.

23: St Mayota, one of the daughters of St Donald (cf 12 July), feasted at Drumoak, south-west of Aberdeen.

25: St Bathan, died *circa* 639, very popular in Berwickshire and East Lothian.

11

Some Customs and Festivals of Winter

This season of wet, murkiness and cold was always a time of fantasy in Scotland, when folk gathered round the ingle-neuks to hear the sagas retold and the folktales recited. It was the time when ghosts walked abroad at the behest of Odin, Lord of the Dead. But to ease the effects of harsh weather it was also a time of feasting and celebration, which began a month or so before the real beginning of astronomical winter, the solstice of 21–22 December. In Scotland the spirits of winter were abroad at . . .

MARTINMAS

St Martin, the fourth-century Bishop of Tours, and tutor of St Ninian, was often pictured on a white horse as the harbinger of snow, and his day, 11 November, was the time the medieval Scots said winter began to intensify. Hew Ainslie set the scene:

> It's dowie in the hint o' hairst,
> At the wa'gang o' the swallow,
> When the wind grows cauld,
> And the burns grow bauld,
> And the woods are hingin' yellow.

The Feast of St Martin was grafted on to old Hallowe'en, and the even older Feast of Hu, whereat oxen were slain to be salted for winter consumption. In many parts of northern Scotland, St Martin's Day was one of rest from work, and it was a quarter-day elsewhere for paying bills, rent and re-hiring domestic and agricultural staff.

During modern times the Feast of St Martin has come to coincide with Armistice Day, the occasion for solemn ceremonials at village, town and city war memorials, in honour of those who fell in wartime. Tradition recalls that the original armistice between Imperial Germany and the Allies, signed at Compiègne, was held at the eleventh hour, of the eleventh day of the eleventh month of 1918.

26 DECEMBER

The Masons' Walk, Melrose
Boxing Day is traditionally that of the Masons' Walk, at Melrose, Roxburghshire. Although St Stephen's Day, in the medieval calendar, it is also the Eve of St John the Apostle and Evangelist, which is celebrated by Masonic Lodges throughout Scotland. Since the 1700s the freemasons of Melrose have gathered at their Lodge to walk in torchlit procession around the Border town's market square, top-hatted and carrying their regalia. At the head of the procession customarily walked the Tyler (the traditional doorkeeper of the Masonic Lodge), with drawn sword; then came the bandsmen, the brethren following two by two, preceding the stewards with their white wands. The standard bearers walked in front of the Bible bearer, who walked alone. Lastly came the Grand Master escorted by his wardens.

Today the torchlit procession leads off to the ruined Cistercian abbey, founded by David I in 1136. Near to the site of the high altar – the reputed resting place of the now-vanished reliquary shrine containing the heart of Robert I, the Bruce – the masons take part in a service. Whereafter they proceed back to their Lodge.

31 DECEMBER

Swinging the Fireballs, Stonehaven
Stonehaven, with its Fetteresso castle, the former home of the Earls Marischal, has long dominated the history and economy of Kincardineshire. At this time of year local folk and visitors still gather to watch an age-old ritual known as the Fireball Ceremony. The fireballs,

which custom dictates should be truly circular, are made up of inflammable material. As the last stroke of midnight peals from the clock tower, the fireballs are set alight and the bearers move off along the High Street whirling the blazing balls in fiery crescents above their heads. Very great dexterity is needed to swing the balls safely, and the parade continues until the balls are almost burned out; then the fragments are scattered on each side of the thoroughfare.

In past centuries the ceremony was designed to ensure prosperity in the coming year and drive away all evil influences. Folklorists believe that some time in the Dark Ages a shooting star appeared above what is now Stonehaven. Thereafter, by coincidence, the tribesmen dwelling nearby may have had bumper crops from land and sea. The seers of the tribe then attributed this prosperity to the coming of the shooting star, so they mimicked the coming of the star annually to assure such prosperity. The fireball custom in its present form dates from around the 1850s, and developed as a fishermen's tradition.

Flambeaux Procession, Comrie, Perthshire

Sir Walter Scott chose the hunting-forest of Glenartney as the opening scene of his *The Lady of the Lake*. Nearby, and standing on the River Earn, the village of Comrie owes its fame to an ancient custom. Records show that the flambeaux custom exhibited some of the aspects of the animal cults of the United Kingdom, with the flambeaux bearers formerly sporting animal horn head-dresses.

As midnight approaches these days, the folk of Comrie assemble in the town square and the flambeaux bearers stand in readiness. The flambeaux, by the by, are enormous flaming torches on eight- to ten-foot poles. As the last stroke of midnight sounds the torches are lit, and to the skirl of the bagpipes the bearers tour the village. On returning to the square the torches are thrown into the middle and people stand around until they have burned away.

No one can be sure how the flambeaux custom originated. Yet, there were tribesmen in the hills around Comrie from long before the days of the Roman legionaries. So it is likely that the custom is a relic of a once potent Celtic fire festival.

12

The Feast of Yule and Scotland's Christmas

The ancient Feast of Yule lasted from 25 December to 6 January, and was named after *Iol*, the Scandinavian festival of the winter solstice in which the sun (at the farthest point south in its celestial journey) was petitioned to return. It was celebrated by the Danes, and then the Norsemen of the far north of Scotland up to the tenth century, at groaning festive tables or wherever they happened to be, as Sir Walter Scott reminded us in 'Marmion':

> Even heathen yet, the savage Dane
> At Iol more deep the mead did drain;
> High on the beach his galleys draw,
> And feasted all the pirate crew.

The main toast was to Thor, although the centrepiece of the feasting board was a boar's head representing Frey, the god of sunshine, who rode the heavens on Gulliburstin, the gold-bristled boar. In time, via the Roman *dies natalis solis invicti* ('the birth day of the unconquered sun' – 25 December), the pagan feast was merged into the Christian Nativity.

When the French influences on the Scottish court were most strong, particularly during the regency of Marie de Guise-Lorraine and the reign of her daughter Mary Queen of Scots, a Continental character entered Scotland's medieval Christmas junketing, namely the Lord of Misrule, also called the Abbot of Unreason. From Hallowmas to Candlemas he held sway at balls, masques and mummeries. He was joined in due time by the Boy Bishop, who capered on Childermas (26 December – Holy Innocents' Day), and who was the festal figure beloved of choirboys and schoolboys. In particular this figure was popular at Dunfermline, the records of 1303 inform us, where the abbey ran a school.

As for Yule, the medieval feast of Christmas in Scotland lasted from Christmas to Uphalieday (6 January), and the period was often referred to as the Daft Days. Every burgh seems to have had its own variations to the festivities. For instance in Cullen, Banff, a piper led a procession to places where games and sports were held, and in Edinburgh the burgesses held family receptions.

In Scotland, New Year has always been a more important secular celebration than Christmas. The reasons for this are undoubtedly twofold. One was the traditional Celtic devotion to the 'turn of the year' ritual, and the other was the Calvinist view that the Feast of the Nativity was 'popish'. The denizens of the Reformed Church charged those who played, danced or sang 'filthy carols on Yule Day' with devil-worship and punished them at Kirk Sessions. This did vary from area to area: in the Covenanting south-west, Yule was largely ignored with the clergy 'spying' on parishioners who might have clandestine festivities, while in the Roman Catholic Highlands and Episcopalian north-east the old festivals were popular. Consequently, traditionally shop hours and employees' holidays were geared towards 'a day at the New Year'. In modern times shops in Scotland are shut both at New Year and Christmas.

Those who did celebrate Christmas in Scotland took their lead from Sir Walter Scott's backward-looking glance at 'Christmas Even in the Olden Time':

> And well our Christmas sires of old
> Loved when the year its course had roll'd,
> And brought blithe Christmas back again,
> With all his hospitable train.
> Domestic and religious rite
> Gave honour to the holy night.

He went on to eulogize the aspects he understood (and therefore liked) of the medieval Christmas – the food, the games, and the carols – and the flickering light of the Yule log's glow. His picture appealed to the Victorian soul, and the 'anglified' Victorian middle classes in Scotland were the first to re-create 'old Christmas'. They sanctified it with a Calvinist double standard and brought the Nativity within the hallowed circle of the hearth. Here in the fire's glint they decorated Christmas and imbued it with new customs and such of the medieval 'popish' traditions as they could swallow.

Following Albert, the Prince Consort's lead at Balmoral, the Christmas tree entered the Scottish living-room. The turkey and crackers were the relics of the Celtic feast, and a toast to Victoria was the new adaptation of the honouring of the tribal female shaman. Christmas developed as a festival of friendship rather than of deep religious significance. Houses were cleaned and refurbished and relations encouraged to call.

The Scottish penchant for cosiness, then, led to a Scottish traditional Christmas centring on the Yule log. A family would collect their logs (or log, as the domestic hearth shrank), and place them in the centre of a peat or coal fire. A candle too was set in the window as a 'torch of welcome'. Mistletoe, once a great healing agent in Scotland (the Gaelic word for it, *nuadhulig*, means 'heal-all'), returned with the Victorians with its accompanying kissing of the Druidic fertility rite. Throughout Scotland, ivy, box, holly, bay and yew were the main Christmas decorations.

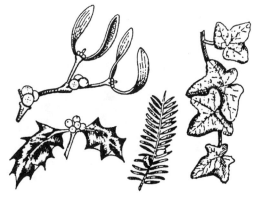

Scotland lays claim to inventing the Christmas card. On 17 December 1841 one Charles Drummond, a publisher and bookseller of Kirkgate, Leith, placed in his shop window a Yuletide greetings card. He is said to have obtained the idea from Thomas Sturrock of Trinity, Edinburgh. The card was engraved by A.T. Aikman, who added a laughing chubby-cheeked boy, and sales escalated over the ensuing years. Christmas cards in Scotland have become more 'religious' in symbolism in modern times, but those containing sprigs of real heather tied with tartan ribbons are still deemed ideal nostalgia for the exiled Scot.

Few of Scotland's own carols survived the Reformation — William Dunbar's 'The Nativitie of Christ' is a notable exception — but many carols of Scottish spirit (some obviously reworkings of ancient verses) appeared in Lewis's *Scottish Presbyterian Eloquence Displayed* (1720). Few Scots have tried their hand at carol composition in modern times. Any individuality which a Scottish Christmas might have had has fast disappeared, and the festivities are almost indistinguishable from those of England.

Index

103